TEXT ME,

Love Mom

TEXT ME,
Love Mom

Two Girls, Two Boys, One Empty Nest

Candace Allan

IGUANA

Copyright © 2014 Candace Allan
Published by Iguana Books
720 Bathurst Street, Suite 303
Toronto, Ontario, Canada
M5V 2R4

Publisher: Greg Ioannou
Editor: Kathryn Willms
Front cover image and design: Shea Proulx
Author photo: Rose Athena
Book layout design: Kate Unrau

Library and Archives Canada Cataloguing in Publication

Allan, Candace, 1959-, author
     Text me, love mom : two girls, two boys, one empty nest /
Candace Allan.

Issued in print and electronic formats.
ISBN 978-1-77180-071-6 (pbk.).--ISBN 978-1-77180-072-3 (epub).--
ISBN 978-1-77180-073-0 (kindle).--ISBN 978-1-77180-074-7 (pdf)

     1. Allan, Candace, 1959-. 2. Empty nesters. 3. Mother and child.
4. Mothers--Psychology. 5. Text messaging (Cell phone systems).
I. Title.

HQ759.43.A55 2014   306.874'3   C2014-904969-2
                                              C2014-904970-6

This is an original print edition of *Text Me, Love Mom*.

I am most grateful to my parents, who raised five of us wisely in the age of free-range children.

I dedicate this story with love to my own four spirited children and to my husband, Mike, the greatest patron of our art. XO

Contents

Prologue... ix

Chapter 1: Much Less Blah, Blah, Blah from Us 1

Chapter 2: Teenage Sympathizer................................... 9

Chapter 3: Like A Rocket Ship 13

Chapter 4: Setting Up Zoë....................................... 18

Chapter 5: It's Not Like I'm A Cry Baby Or Anything 25

Chapter 6: Snowboard Boy's First Suit.......................... 34

Chapter 7: Gap or Gorge?....................................... 38

Chapter 8: Twigs and Sticks and Bits of String................. 51

Chapter 9: Frozen Toothpaste Spit 57

Chapter 10: Sketchy Times 62

Chapter 11: Show Me Your Feathers 77

Chapter 12: The Unbearable Weight of Being Misunderstood . 90

Chapter 13: Lost Down Under 130

Chapter 14: Text Me, Mr. Tambourine Man 138

Chapter 15: Teenage Runaway 146

Chapter 16: A New Chapter 166

Chapter 17: The House Halfway Up the Hill 183

Epilogue: Two Years Slip By 197

Disclaimer:

Every name has been changed and the events depicted went mostly like this…

Prologue

Ancient writers believed that the mother bear continually licked her little cub until it took shape. This was considered to be the very essence of creation, and as a result the Greeks and Romans referred to the bear only in the feminine gender.

— *"The Bear Facts,"* Association of Zoos and Aquariums

Your father and I dated, I tell our kids, for seven years before we married. Saying it, I wonder, what does *dated* mean? In May 1977, Will caught up to me in our high school hallway to ask what I was doing that night. When I admitted that I was reading my poetry at a gallery called Clouds and Water, he asked if he could take me there. That was our first date and then I think we were *going out.*

We went out for two years before we shacked up. After much cajoling, my parents consented to my moving to Toronto to take a creative writing degree that wasn't available at home in Calgary. Going back to school wasn't on Will's radar yet, but he was happy to pack up his collection of albums — Led Zeppelin, Pink Floyd, Billy Joel, and Fleetwood Mac — and to ship his new stereo and larger-than-life speakers to Toronto to be my roommate in a tiny North York apartment. For a couple of twenty-year-olds from Calgary, it was a pretty sexy adventure. I wrote essays, he got a lousy job in the Sears toy department, and we bickered about important things like who was going to do the laundry this month so that we could go back to wearing underwear.

I kept a little ledger in those days, and when I bought a loaf of bread, I'd tell him he owed me twenty-five cents and, oh yeah, that plastic dish rack was $3.99, but he could take his half off what I owed for last night's Hawaiian pizza. It was okay in my mind to be in debt to my parents or the bank, but, damn it, I wasn't going to owe or lend fifty cents to my boyfriend. And yet, despite my initial resistance to co-dependency and my two years of feminist studies classes (in which I wrote essays about the unequal division of household labour), I still wanted Will to ask me to marry him and assumed that we would have children together. On a summer evening in 1983, the year I finished my degree, he took me to our bench in Glenmore Park above the city reservoir and presented me with a floral teapot. I held my breath and looked up at a tiny slip of moon. Years earlier, I had told him how my dad proposed to my mom by presenting her with a diamond ring in a china teapot. Sure enough, I opened it to find an engagement ring tinkling around in the bottom.

We wed having never discussed the number of babies we wanted, when we'd want to be graced by their arrival, or even practical considerations like how we were going to afford them. My insistence on splitting the cost of every loaf of bread had long since been abandoned. When I became pregnant with our first, Will was in the last months of an undergraduate degree before three years of law school. His student loan coffers were being supplemented through assistance from our parents, my paycheques from a waitressing gig, and the promise of proceeds from the great Canadian novel I planned to write, with the expertise of my Creative Writing degree, while our little one napped. Our more practical friends thought our timing was off, yet I recall feeling a biological urge to have that baby that couldn't be undone by a calendar or a budget. My parents and parents-in-law were worried, but in 1983, no one was putting our rash behaviour down to being too young.

In today's climate of extended adolescence and emerging adulthood, mine would seem almost a teenage pregnancy. I know young women today who don't plan to have babies until they are pushing forty, even though the media increasingly warns us of the fertility risks of putting off those childbearing years. Back in 1984, my girlfriends who had the nerve to accuse me of reproducing prematurely only took another year or two before they got serious about their reproductive planning. Should their baby be born in early summer to avoid an overheated pregnancy? Or May to make their child the ideal age when they commenced kindergarten?

Will and I were never that calculating. I always told my four kids, you were all planned. You were just planned really, really quickly. Needless to say, my visions of quiet afternoons writing while the baby slept were quickly shattered by reality. The arrival of Zoë knocked our collective socks off. It was a heroic feat to keep my eyes open, shower periodically, tend to every last one of her little baby needs, and get over lingering earth mother intentions like making homemade baby food. One afternoon, I watched a couple walk past holding the hands of their small boy and swinging him happily off the ground between them. I remember thinking, that picture looks just right — two adults, one child. A week later, I was pregnant with my second baby. Our family would make a slightly bigger mosaic.

Our second child, Cole, was, and still is, the polar opposite of his introspective sister, Zoë. At nine months, he was running figure eights around the three of us. A friend's daughters giggled whenever they saw him and called him the bad baby. I never, ever saw him fall asleep. He conked out in private.

In the midst of that chaos, I had a feeling I couldn't shake. During a desperately needed weekend escape, looking out at the starry night from a window of the rundown Waterton Lakes Park Hotel, I told my husband, We can discuss whether or not we should have a third, but I just know there's another one waiting to come to us. We brought our third child, Hudson, home from the hospital on a damp late December evening after stopping to pick up a Christmas tree. A perfect gift.

Hudson, unlike his brother Cole, was always up for a cuddle; in fact, his preferred mode of transportation was balancing on my hip. At the tender age of only three-and-a-half, Zoë was in training to be a mother's helper for her two brothers, but I couldn't help but feel that I was falling behind the eight ball on some mothering particulars. On one of my I-can-only-open-one-eye mornings, I found her at the fridge filling Cole's bottle with milk and getting another bottle ready for herself. If I had missed introducing Zoë to the sippy cup in my overwhelmed state, what else had I neglected?

It turns out that I had neglected to give Zoë a sister. I was pregnant again. With Hudson, the cuddler, wanting to be close, Cole rappelling off the furniture, and Zoë absorbed with her colouring book like a miniature Emily Carr, I was stealing the odd hour to write. Sitting at my computer while Hudson, comfy and warm in the Snugli, helped stoke my creative energy, I experienced a moment of escape from scrubbing Kool-Aid off the floors, picking Cheerios out of the car seats, and cooking copious numbers of eggs-in-a-hole.

Will was admitted to the Alberta Bar to begin his career as a lawyer. I should have been admitted to the loony bin for not being content with anything less than this new family montage: me with new baby, Lily, in the Snugli, two-year-old Hudson bumping along on my hip, as little Cole ran reconnaissance and Zoë helped push the empty buggy. For years after, there were still moments in the shower when I debated whether or not I could accept that I was finished with babies — the teeny soft heads and chubby feet. I missed kissing that spot under their wobbly necks, not to mention their gurgles, and the sweetness of their sugar breaths when they were tucked into bed with us. Was I done with all of that? It was telling that these moments of longing occurred in the shower, the only place or time I had for reflection. Four was enough.

I was a young mom, although I didn't always feel that way. We made it through those early years intact. All of these cooing babies, and then whining toddlers, became boisterous teens who filled our home and hearts, and consumed my time, patience, and energy. While our friends negotiated over-the-top children's birthday parties, Will and I were surviving hip hop concerts in the basement and guarding against teens-gone-wild. For years and years, I never thought much about them moving out of our home and how my heart would deal with that. It was what we were preparing them for — the launch from the nest. In the middle of it all, it was hard to believe it would ever happen.

I was only forty-three when my eldest daughter left our chaotic home in Calgary.

Were my parents just as stunned and confused to have a child slipping out of their grasp and away from their influence? The media would have us believe that we have overindulged, overprotected, and over-parented our kids. Could this explain why I suffered from the jitters when one by one, all too quickly, my children dispersed and I desperately wished I could visit my local pharmacist and buy a patch to help ease me off them? I was looking for a chemical that could simulate the sound of cellphones chirping incessantly or of the front door creaking and a movie downloading at two a.m. Or maybe something that would produce the same irritation I felt at the sight of their messy rooms or the sensation of pleasure when one of them slowed down long enough to wrap their arms around me in a hug.

When my children struck out on their own, I was bewildered. I felt like the mother bear I had seen in a film whose cub had been taken away too early. She had rolled her head from side to side and clumped through the forest in a distressed fashion. Learning to deal with my first strayed cub, my heart pounded, my sleep was uneven, and I couldn't concentrate to complete a task.

My kids say I could start my own lending library with my vast collection of parenting tomes, yet there was a void of information to guide me through these turbulent times — starting with that spring day that my daughter was accepted to university in another province and I realized I had worked myself out of a position with which I was damn comfortable. That void inspired this book.

They left home in the order they were born. Not enough time passed between Zoë, the oldest, moving out and Lily, the baby, phoning from a crowded European city to tell me how hard it was to find a place to cry out loud, the way she preferred to cry. Back up, you kids, I thought. I want to run through that all again. But no, we're going forward.

Chapter 1

Much Less Blah, Blah, Blah from Us

I think I can fly. If I can just get high enough, I think I can fly.

– Zoë, age five

It was the way it was supposed to happen. Your kids grow up and leave home. All my friends, with their kids still tucked under their roofs, said so. I just wasn't ready to think of Zoë as particularly grown-up. "You need to chill out, Mom," sixteen-year-old Cole told me. "There will still be three of us here to drive you crazy."

Hudson looked up from his peanut butter toast. "Word," he said. "And you have Lily. Lily will stay home forever." Back then, I imagined that sensitive, particular Lily would stay put for a while — how foolish.

Letting our eighteen-year-old eldest move away from home before *I* was ready was freaking me out so much that, on a late spring day, I drove to the local big box bookstore, bought a comforting latte, and sought out a clerk to ask whether there existed, in their colossal parenting section, a book on helping your kids go away to school. Asking the question caused my voice to squeak embarrassingly with emotion, which I wasn't able to hide from the elderly woman clicking her tongue as she scrolled through the store's computer. Her kids would have left home eons ago. She would be *so* over it. The books she led me to were instruction guides on how to choose universities — forcing me to clear my throat and address her confusion. *No, what I really need is a book for me. I'm having trouble dealing with her leaving home.* I was so visibly on the verge of coming undone that she searched harder and found me the volume that became my coping bible, *Ophelia's Mom: Loving and Letting Go of Your Adolescent Daughter.* My eyes riveted to the back cover description of women writing about "how the changes in their daughters' lives are prompting cataclysm in their own." *Catalytic* — now they were talking.

I wasn't honest with Zoë about my issues with her leaving. I didn't want her to have to deal with that on top of everything else. I had always made a point of being more open with her, sharing where I was at emotionally. It was something my own mom hardly ever did. Not because she didn't want to. She just couldn't; she didn't have the words.

I had the words. Zoë would patiently listen and nod, hardly ever arguing with whatever I asked of her (unlike my other three more combative children). But what *was* I asking of her as she filled out university applications? *Don't grow up. I can't bear for you to leave this nest.*

Zoë was setting out to pursue her artistic goals. I understood that; I had those, too. Somewhere along the zigzagging road of life, I had decided that I could raise a family *and* be a writer. If the writing wasn't going well, I compensated by focusing on my family. Not on the day-to-day activities like laundry or making dinners more creative than chicks-in-a-hole (tear a hole in a piece of bread, crack an egg into it in a buttery frying pan, and — yummy — mommy's outdone herself again). It was more like me, the North American helicopter mom, to obsess over my four kids' iffy social skills and lack of attention to school work, or whether their latest crushes had damaged their psyches. The three youngest are better at keeping me at a distance, though they've *all* given me reason to lie in bed at night fretting and imagining my hair going gray under its latest colour job. But Zoë was the first to struggle through teenage angst and I worried about her.

"Mom, I'll be eighteen in July," she admonished me. "I'll be okay." As if on the eve of that birthday she'd be sprinkled with fairy dust and metamorphose into a socially at-ease creature. She felt bravely ready to leave home, but I wasn't so sure. Had I prepared her? How would she survive without her family backing her up? Zoë was threatening to fly the nest while I was still taking care of her needs. That was a wake-up call for me: I had to at least teach her a few sustenance-gathering tricks. My most fretful concerns, however, had nothing to do with her ability to feed herself (okay — I did worry about how horribly thin she might get). What kept me awake listening to her dad's uneven snoring was my perception that she wasn't ready to be out there mixing it up with a whole wide world of folks — a school community and the entire metropolis of Vancouver — without the shelter of *us*. I worried about how well she read other people, especially the not-to-be-trusted sort. I was anxious about her dating strangers, boys who hadn't snuck a Heineken from our refrigerator or played eight ball in our basement.

I listened to Zoë's girlfriends whine about not having boyfriends and silently observed how they all seemed to lust after some already-spoken-for lover boy or the sad, shy guys who couldn't break out of their shells. I surprised myself by advising that they try to have more fun, not to take it all so damn seriously. Couldn't they just make out with someone now and then, because they were young and, face it, kissing is fun? After all, wasn't this generation much more playful with their sexualities than mine was? What hadn't changed was that the girls still gave something up each time they were intimate, while the boys felt pressure to appear annoyingly casual. I worried about Zoë getting her heart broken.

I had yet to read Laura Sessions Stepp's book *Unhooked: How Young Women Pursue Sex, Delay Love and Lose at Both*. She delves into the contemporary adolescent culture of *hooking up*, with its defining characteristic being the ability to unhook from a partner at any time. Her argument is that young women can't transform hook-up buddies into serious boyfriends because they don't know how to get to that next level. When I did read *Unhooked*, Zoë's younger sister, Lily, had to put up with my attempts to involve her in animated discussion, because *Mom was onto some new parenting hype again.* My boys were even less willing participants in these discussions, and Cole insisted the looseness of hook-up culture was what many of the girls he knew were after. So, though I lacked the terminology back then, I did worry about Zoë and *hooking up.*

Zoë has been described as having her head in the clouds. But this is a careless misunderstanding of my daughter. She's often astray because she is *so* earth bound, trying to memorize the sloped lines around a person's eyes or the pattern a twisted caterpillar makes on a rotted bit of stick. Before she left home, I wanted her to know that she could see the world through an artist's eyes, but she shouldn't hide in her art. She had to engage herself and be aware of what's going on around her. *Art* can be a lonely place and you have to come out of it sometimes to connect.

A close friend confided that she wanted her kids to stay home and go to our local university or college for the first two years, and after that, they could choose to go further afield. Brilliant idea, I thought, but our negotiations had already advanced beyond that. Will and I were frustrated by Zoë's impatience with the idea of going to school in Calgary, though *we* were the ones guilty of putting the option of going elsewhere on the table. But saying you can go away to university is not the same as saying, *I am ready to no longer see you coming through the back alley on your way home from school. I can handle your bed staying made day after day after day.* Of course, it was possible that Zoë wouldn't get into Emily Carr, the west coast art school in

4

Vancouver, BC, that she had her heart set on. Whatever happened, I knew I would have to change. I *knew* that. I had to give her more freedom. Could I keep my mouth shut more often? Was it possible to convince her that there would be nothing wrong with living at home longer, that she could still grow and learn here while having her friends over to yak and make nachos at three a.m.? Could I actually make her believe that if she did stay, we would give her more liberty to carry on her affairs with much less *blah, blah, blah* from us? Instead of a noisy helicopter, I told myself I could be a *glider*, quietly observing, rarely interfering. Honestly, Zoë, I would do that, I thought. Just don't go quite yet. Nobody leaves home at eighteen anymore, do they?

It was a misty June afternoon — a summer storm had blown through, stirring up the scent of lilac in the yard, and the sun was just reappearing behind gray clouds — when I learned, before Zoë, that she *had* been accepted to the Emily Carr University of Art and Design in Vancouver. I hadn't opened the envelope addressed to her — I would never have done that. And I wouldn't have been able to see through it holding it up to the light. It had one of those windows though, so when I scrunched the envelope just so, I could see enough to know that it was their *pleasure* to tell my daughter that she had been accepted into their foundation year. I cried. I'd been imagining myself crying and I didn't let me down. Through my tears, I noticed that, far to the south east, a rainbow had appeared. I am a sucker for omens: spilled salt over the left shoulder, lucky coins on the road, first sightings of robins, and four leaf clovers in the lawn. Not all the colours in the rainbow were discernible — the red blended into orange and the yellow barely tipped to green. I saw deep blue, but not indigo or violet, stretched across the horizon. Still, I was certain it was a sign of good fortune for Zoë and her future at school. It would be okay. Of course, it would.

I had been delighted for Zoë when she applied for art school. She wanted this so much and I had made sure to talk with her, late one night sitting on the edge of her bed, about how if they didn't select her, she shouldn't see it as a measure of the worth of her art (which she poured her whole spirit into). I knew rejection would feel absolutely devastating to my soulful daughter. I told her it might just be three or four tired people looking at portfolio after portfolio with hundreds of pieces as wonderful and ambitious as her work. You can't let it get you down if they don't let you in, I had said (though, I was thinking, it will be insane if they don't recognize your ridiculous talent).

Then again, I was aware that if they failed to see her full and exciting potential and refused her, *my* fluttering heart could be still. I would hold her and buffer her ego, encouraging her to be positive about staying home with us and going to school in our city, where she had already been accepted. And I could put all this worry behind me.

Heck, two years previous, when she was finishing tenth grade and had first started considering art schools, I dreamt out loud with her that she could go to the Sorbonne in Paris. Paris, for God's sake. In my muddled, wacky, *my-child-can-do-anything* mind, I pictured her wearing a jaunty beret over her brunette ponytail, setting up her easel on the banks of the Seine. That must have come from reading too much Hemingway. But Hemingway was a full grown man with his poor long-suffering wife and Gertrude Stein looking out for him. This was my itsy-bitsy daughter and, yes, it was Vancouver we were now talking about, just a short flight away, but I had fear written all over my face and she hadn't even seen the scrunched envelope yet.

The family was divided on Zoë leaving. Twelve-year-old Lily didn't want her big sister to go away. Hudson, two years older than Lily, had always hated change. He didn't even like it when we got rid of an old couch, let alone his sister. On the other hand, Cole, at sixteen, was already imagining himself hanging out in his sister's Vancouver apartment. Zoë's dad and I both had the jitters about her leaving and had separately engaged her in *logical* conversations about how it might not be the best plan, how she needed to be aware of the expense, and how we would give her more freedom in our house if she stayed (though the neighbours on either side must have wondered how much more free this house of teens could get). But there I was, sitting on the back steps with the scrunched envelope in hand and tears slipping down my cheeks. All of our interventions had been for naught; it was actually happening.

I'd been shoving chipped dishes and discarded furniture into the *for-the-kids-when-they-move-out* half of the garage for some time. But as I got up from the back steps and started to face reality, I was imagining the trip to Ikea to pick out the complete (hopefully cheap) furnishings for a cool student apartment. The university didn't have a residence, and if we were going to let Zoë leave home, we wouldn't settle for her sharing an apartment with any of the Tom, Dick, or Harrys (or Lindsey, Ashley, and Britneys) who might advertise for roommates.

She could room temporarily with good friends of ours who had two young children and lived in North Vancouver — a long trek to the school. It would be nothing like living in our house where on a typical Friday night, the kids would have their friends over. The energy of all those twelve to eighteen-year-olds in the heat of first crushes or the agonies of unreturned (or unnoticed) love created an audible buzz. The house would smell like popcorn and melted nacho cheese, mixed with the peppery scent of adolescent hormones. The party mood was contagious enough to make me want to apply fresh hair colour, wipe on the *skin regenerating* cream, kick off my Clarks, and get down to a tickle fight with my hubby. We usually settled for pizza and a movie while we patrolled the teen zone in the basement.

If we let her go, was it possible that Zoë would meet some nice kids who had never done crack or pierced their genitals, and they would live together in a well-organized house just rambunctious enough to be the setting for a *Friends* episode? Maybe one of her new friends' parents would live in Vancouver — wealthy, philanthropic people who allowed their kids to have apartments in their own city — and would invite Zoë for hearty Sunday family dinners, in case she didn't eat all week, and let her do her laundry in their state-of-the-art machines.

What I feared, of course, is that she would move in with a shoddy bunch of eccentric artists who had gone far beyond body piercing, wouldn't even *have* parents, and would hardly let me darken their doorstep, even when I arrived with a U-Haul full of chipped dishes and faded furniture (because with the cost of living in Vancouver, that trip to Ikea might be a fantasy).

I knew what those west coast people were like. If I didn't visit often so as to continue to gently influence her, Zoë was liable to take up with a vegan, nudist meditation instructor who would encourage her to ditch us because of our loose ties to the energy sector, even if it was paying for her education and trashy apartment, not to mention her laptop and printer.

On that sunny afternoon in June, I was the only one to have glimpsed her future. I had to erase the fear from my face before she arrived with a carload of friends. Perfectly good friends, I might add, not vegan nudists. I had to wipe the slate of my imagination clean. Let my not-quite-eighteen-year-old Zoë feel that the world was her oyster — at least for the few seconds it took her to read the scrunched letter. They wanted her and that was truly wonderful. But, damn it, we wanted her, too.

Chapter 2

Teenage Sympathizer

*I see no hope for the future of our people if they are
dependent on the frivolous youth of today, for certainly all
youth are reckless beyond words. When I was a boy, we were
taught to be discrete and respectful of elders, but the present
youth are exceedingly wise and impatient of restraint.*

– Hesiod, Eighth Century BC

So Zoë, at just barely eighteen-years-old, was going away to
school in another province. It was time to grow up, but I didn't
know if I could. I liked being a hip mom, but this situation called
for maturity. I just didn't see myself as old enough for all of this. I
wanted to be giving Zoë a ride to piano lessons, not the airport. I
liked having a house full of teens — most days. If I was going to
stop sobbing and grabbing onto her arm during long distance
commercials (funny — those still existed a few years back), I
needed a new view of myself, not of Zoë.

One Wednesday late in June, Will arrived home and politely
inquired as to why so many of Zoë's friends were gathered in our

backyard again. He had yet to notice that the boys were in their boxers. Forever a teenage sympathizer, I handed him the ice for his drink and said calmly, "Some of them just wrote their last exam. I think they're feeling celebratory. Let them be."

"Will there be another party when the *rest of them* write their last exam?"

"Seriously, Dad, this isn't a party," Zoë told him, wrapping a towel around her bikini-clad body. "It's just a few of my friends celebrating a bit."

Zoë's a good kid. If it *were a party*, she would certainly have let us know. Eight kids having a water fight, with the boys in boxers and the ones of age knocking back a few beers, followed by a session of whipping up nachos in the oven accompanied by rap music, was definitely *not* a party.

Just then, two of the more manly looking boys skidded by the kitchen window in their boxers and socks. As Zoë's dad leapt out the deck door to grab them — not that there was much to grab them by — I became a full blown supporter of their... *youthful charm.* "Come on. Come on. They just finished high school. Twelve years. Of course, they're giddy." Lily and her friend, Heidi, waved at Will from their post in our dilapidated tree house. The younger girls looked entertained, as if they had balcony seats to a reality TV show.

Will waved back at Lily and Heidi but yelled at the others to get dressed or *all thunder* would break loose. They might have been unfamiliar with that expression, but the guys rushed back into their jeans. Will stepped back inside to demand further explanation. "Wasn't there a party for this already?" he asked Zoë. He turned to me. "Didn't they call it graduation? Wasn't that the night we spent a zillion bucks dressing Zoë up so she could sit at a banquet for two hours, have three dances, and then change back into her street clothes in a washroom cubicle like a superhero, before vanishing for the real celebration out of our sight? Furthermore, wasn't there a party here three days later, after we watched five hundred of them march across the stage?" His excitement was elevating to match theirs. "And what the heck was *last* Friday? Wasn't there a whole lot of teens in a celebratory mood here then, too?"

"Oh, Dad, *that* was the last day of *classes*. Cole's friends were here, too."

Will pointed to a tall boy from four doors up the road. "Cole's friends are here now, if I'm not mistaken."

"Dad, you can't count Jacob," Zoë said. Jacob, Cole's closest friend, was now helping to distribute the nachos. He was almost a member of our family, but then that was true of Hudson's pals, Robin and Mark, from around the block, and Lily's entourage of blonde twelve-year-olds — Heidi and Charlotte, who were Jacob and Robin's sisters, and Mattie from across the street. This was a popular strategy with our kids — pointing out that the number of friends that each of them has over isn't that out of line — say two or three a piece — resulting in Friday nights with a dozen or more kids sprawled about the house.

"That was the last day of classes," Zoë explained again to her clueless father. *"This* is the last day of *exams...*" She lowered her voice and stuffed a nacho into her mouth, mumbling, "... at least for some people." Zoë and a few others still had four more days before their last exam and then it would be *their* turn to be giddy and celebratory... and in their underwear.

"You see," I said, "maybe this is the universe's plan to help us let her go. If they drive us insane over the summer, it will be easier to separate." I choked on the s-word. I really did need to grow up. I needed to be a Shirley Partridge type of mom, hip but mature enough to set some rules, take back the stereo and put on some Fleetwood Mac instead of *Bowling For Soup*, and take her shopping for school supplies and a sensible raincoat. As a responsible mom, I would study tourist guides of Vancouver with her and teach her how to grocery shop for ripe melons and reasonable cuts of meat.

But I wasn't ready for all that. There was something magical about the summer after high school. I felt more like Lorelai Gilmore, the mother-as-friend from television's *Gilmore Girls*, than my generation's sensible Shirley Partridge (then again, she was a singer in a pop band). The moods of the kids around us were contagious. At that point, we still had Zoë's eighteenth birthday party to plan, as well as some sort of big family gathering before she officially went away. Forget the grocery shopping lessons, bring on the nachos, I thought, kicking off my Clarks so I could skid across the grass and take a run through the sprinkler.

Chapter 3

Like A Rocket Ship

Zoë used to have a quote by Yeats circling her bedroom wall. It read, "Tread softly because you tread on my dreams." I have to admit now that this past summer her aspirations have driven me so crazy, it's been a feat not to have tread on them. But here it is September and I've done it. I've let her go spinning away from me, right out of the nest.

– Personal journal entry, Sept. 15, 2002

When Zoë left home, her copies of *Love In the Time of Cholera*, *Harry Potter*, and *Dragonquest* gone from the shelves, her colorful collection of shoes gathered from the closets, and her vanilla-scented products stripped from the bathroom, I searched the self-help sections for a manual on how to let go. Now that I'm a true empty nest-er, it seems a bit odd. After all, I still had three hyped-up teens in the house. One of them leaving home should have given me a little more room to breathe. But it didn't. It took my breath away.

Zoë had a fast-paced summer. How could she not have? She had a new romance going with a nice guy, not to mention a graduation party (her dad started calling that over-the-top affair her coronation), end-of-school parties, her eighteenth birthday party, and *it-is-a-beautiful-summer-night-and-my-parents-are-suckers* parties. There *was* a lot of celebrating taking place on our back deck — just ask the neighbours — but we didn't mind so much. We knew we were going to miss her friends, too, though we had Cole's, Hudson's, and Lily's crews waiting to take over.

Our Vancouver friends graciously invited her to land with them early enough to attend the university's orientation. As fate would have it, a tenant was vacating an apartment they owned much closer to the university and they offered to rent it to Zoë, but she would need to find a roommate to make the proposal work. So there we were with a new source of anxiety: the mystery of the unknown roomie. It was Vancouver, after all. We had to be on alert for vegan, nudist yoga gurus. I flew out when classes started (okay, I'll confess — I tagged along for the first day of school but only to help out with the roommate hunt. Be patient with me — I got better at all this). With the aid of the exceptional receptionist at Emily Carr University, we found *Anna from Winnipeg*, who was also searching for a roommate. Thankfully, she ate meat. I flew back to Calgary to pack up pots, pans, and cooking utensils to add to the pile of recycled furniture we were going to haul out to the new apartment, though I had to wonder: would Zoë and Anna the carnivore cook or would they exist on a diet of Zoë's preferred fare — handfuls of dry cereal, sesame bagels, and cream cheese?

I hadn't had an opportunity to miss my eldest daughter yet, because I was on my way back to spend a week helping her get set up. I convinced myself that she just couldn't comprehend how much time these organizational projects warranted when she sighed heavily and said, "Really, Mom? Another week?"

My Calgary mom friends were watching this process closely. "Hey," I told them, a wee bit defensively, "there's a lot to do out there." Her dad had to return home right away, but I needed time to set up the internet, arrange for the unlimited long distance land line, and figure out how Zoë would manage without *me*, her manager. As for flying back home when my week was up, I just wasn't going to think about that. Breathe slowly was my mantra. Breathe very slowly.

I was privy to Zoë's eighteen-year-old thoughts and perspective on leaving home in a surprising way. They were broadcast to me over the radio in Zoë's own voice. I had proposed to CBC Radio (Canada's national broadcaster) a few short segments about my daughter leaving home at the time of year when kids across the country were heading off to university and college programs. When a CBC program director called my cell and offered to approve my pitch, I leaned back against the pasta aisle in the grocery store to concentrate on what she was saying. She had an intriguing caveat to my work going on air — they wanted me to convince Zoë to write and contribute her student perspective as well. I'd had short fiction pieces broadcast previously on the radio, presented by trained professionals. This time, they wanted us to come to their studios, me in Calgary and Zoë in Vancouver, and present the work ourselves.

Zoë loved being on air. Me, not so much. Sitting in Calgary's CBC studio before the large microphone, my impulse was to press my sweaty fingers against my temples to suppress a nervous headache, though I tried to look far more relaxed than I felt. The taping wasn't live so the producer was calm as he told me to repeat a paragraph, emphasize this word, not that, try to be less breathy, and go back to the top just one more time.

"Isn't it frustrating?" I asked Zoë over the phone the day we did our recordings in two different provinces.

"Frustrating?" Zoë was nonplussed.

"You know, when you have to repeat it so often to get it the way they want."

"I guess," she said, being polite. "I didn't really repeat much. They said I was good at it."

Of course, they did.

In a clear, confident voice, sounding almost like she was having fun, Zoë read out her response to my tale of letting my first kid leave the nest. Her take on it went something like this:

My mom is obsessed. She's never going to give me a chance to miss her. She thinks she's been helping me organize myself, but really she's been seeking a cure. It's a classic case of first-out-of-the-nest syndrome. This malady has caused her to freak out over the most meaningless details of my new life here, like the optimum positioning of cheap Ikea candles and throw pillows she bought for me. As for the real issues, I think I'm dealing with them quite fine all by myself.

First things first, I've found a roommate. I was scared that the only people still looking were available solely because no one else wanted them. But Anna's really nice. Not too neat and conservative, but not a party animal either. Her mom seems just as loving and insanely hyper-vigilant about sending her off as mine. After Anna and her mom toured the apartment, the mothers immediately started tearing up. Soon they were gabbing like loons, reminiscing over their child raising years with a fondness that only distance allows. They even hugged each other goodbye. Anna and I shared a knowing look and casually shook hands.

It has been handy having Mom around for some practical matters, I guess, but even there she's only got a certain skill set. Mom took transit with me the first day of school and had no idea what she was doing. The woman hadn't gotten on a bus in years, so the world of tickets, transfers, and fare validations was messing her up. I was pretty much guiding her around.

She had stayed close by while I went to orientation, and was already chatting up a storm with my new roommate when I came to meet her. I could tell already that Mom would be ecstatic about this girl, not because she seemed so nice, which she did, or because she was so polite, which she was, but because Anna and I were wearing the exact same jacket. Both of us had on, for all intents and purposes, identical red hoodies. I knew Mom would see this as a sign that we were destined to live together, that it was written in the stars.

My mom has been saying things like this my whole life, but it seemed to me that the signs from the spirits were coming ever more frequently this summer. She kept talking about things falling into place and found omens everywhere — falling stars during a meteor shower, frogs on a pathway. It was true, the apartment did practically fall into our laps, and maybe sighting the neighbourhood three-legged cat more than usual this summer *was* lucky. But mostly my mother needs to believe that in her absence, someone or something's watching over me. And, honestly, maybe it would take a supernatural force to replace her.

Which leaves me wondering, in the words of the enigmatic Clint Eastwood character, Dirty Harry, *Do I feel lucky?*

Chapter 4

Setting Up Zoë

Ladybug, ladybug, fly away home.
Your house is on fire, your children alone.

Setting up Zoë was the tranquil phrase I used to describe the purpose of my trip to Vancouver, but the trip didn't start out calmly. Her dad and grandpa piled the furniture and household goods we'd collected for her into our truck. Inside the house, I unplugged the old toaster to donate to the pile and tugged the quilt her great-grandmother made her off her bed. We hauled it all up over the Rockies and down the Coquihalla Highway, pausing for a late A&W supper in the town of Hope. How fitting for those myriad Canadians who flock to Vancouver, optimistic about the possibilities of a fresh start and new outlook, to have to coast down from the mountain peaks into this aptly-named small town. (They filmed Rambo: First Blood there, and if anyone needed hope, Rambo did.) It is common to fuel up, eat a burger, or take a break from a Greyhound bus ride in Hope. Will, good man that he is, could see that just being in Hope, with that stacked truck of wares for our daughter's new life, was giving me the jitters and gave my hand a squeeze before we sped off across the flat, wet terrain toward Vancouver. As we rolled past a number of vineyards, Will filled the cab with vague facts about drainage, fermentation, and photosynthesis. My panicking thoughts were elsewhere. It occurred to me that during eighteen years of raising my daughter, I'd failed to teach her to make gravy.

Zoë was comfortable in our North Vancouver friends' home while she waited for us to bring furniture and household necessities for the apartment they were going to rent her. We picked her up at their house along with the keys to her new abode. Heading across the Burrard Street Bridge to meet Anna in the apartment lobby, I confessed to Zoë my shortcomings as a mother.

"Don't worry, Mom," she said. "I don't like gravy."

She sympathetically patted my head from the crew cab behind me.

"But some day you may be called upon to make it," I insisted.

"The person calling upon me will have to do it themselves. Gravy is disgusting — grease and flour and water poured over your food. Yuk."

How consoling — she knew the ingredients.

"Relax, Mommy," she said. (My kids stopped calling me Mommy when they were five or six, but my daughters took it up again as teens when they needed to placate me.) "I can always phone you when I need help — like, say, if I *wanted* to make gravy. If I can't get you, I can Google what I need. You can Google anything."

We filled the freight elevator twice, and then Zoë and her dad stood on the corner of West 16th and Elma Street — just a dad and kid in Vancouver, beside a truck with Alberta plates — having a long hug. It seemed to go on forever.

As Will headed back toward Hope, and then the mountains, I imagined *my* stay would be much more relaxed than his brief, panicked one, with time for meditative walks along the wide bay of Kits Beach. A bit of a holiday from the rush of life at home. In fact, I was irritatingly busy with long to-do lists that read thus: call internet provider; call hydro; call *back* internet provider; call telephone company; call and pretend to sob to internet provider dispatcher, etc. Then there were other crucial tasks: buy shower curtain, buy garbage containers, buy favourite bottle of wine, buy corkscrew, buy clothes hangers — try not to think about the hangers that are reproducing like rabbits at home while I fork over hard cash for them in Vancouver — and buy another bottle of vino.

Away from our frenzied family home, which was desperately in need of de-cluttering and reorganization, I found Zoë's apartment Zenlike in its simplicity. We had joined gaggles of parents and students scribbling down names like Bjerk and Wojerk with teeny wooden pencils at Ikea, so as to complete her place with that student/Swedish ambiance. "It's *your* place," I told her, losing the struggle to keep my opinions to myself, "but I would be a minimalist if I were you." Who could deny my credentials in the design field given the two years I had studied *Canadian House and Home* prior to the first renovation of our 1963-era split-level in Calgary? Zoë and Anna preferred a shabby-chic-bohemian art student flare, and every parenting instinct told me shut up. Still, while I wasn't a Dorothy Draper or Frank Lloyd Wright, I knew the burgundy-striped pillow would make the denim blue of the futon couch "pop" better than it did the beige of Grandpa's cast-off easy chair. The girls were oblivious to the sneaky switcheroo I did with the positioning of the art deco paper lantern and the Ikea *Kvart* candle holder. Both of them were focused on school work — mixing smelly oil paint swatches at the kitchen table, chasing *full chroma,* and *discord,* while they giggled over how hard it was not to blush in their figure drawing classes when the live models adjusted their *junk.* When they weren't making flash cards for Western Art History pop quizzes (which came first — the Coliseum or the Pantheon?), they were in their bedrooms with doors shut jabbering with friends in Calgary and Winnipeg — after we finally worked out the unlimited long distance. Honestly, I didn't mind running about and getting things hooked up and turned on, except for my interactions with the Tier Two Internet Problem Solver which had reduced me to a frustrated babbling person about to go over the edge. Thankfully, the Tier Two guy swiftly picked up on my fragile state and delivered Jason-the-wonder-technician to our doorstep.

Did I say *our* doorstep? Was I reliving my youth that transparently? Before my visit, I had suspected that after seven days, my sweet Zoë and I might get fed up with each other. In our previous existence in Calgary, amidst the mad dance of activities of six busy people, there was little time for us to get in each other's way. Although it is *possible* that Zoë was eager to finally be on her own in Vancouver, I never got fed up with her. Okay, maybe I got a *tiny* bit annoyed — *a wee bit bitchy* — that she spent more time on the phone chatting with her Calgary boyfriend and girlfriends than she did conversing with her slightly disturbed mom.

The *real* trouble was that a peculiar phenomenon was occurring as I wandered along, peeling off a sweater to feel the afternoon sun on my bare arms, stopping for a dynamite sushi roll or an iced latte, or climbing on the number ninety-nine bus with noisy students. I was having an identity crisis. Instead of forty-three, *I* felt eighteen. I'd pass by a little grocer or a thrift shop, and think, perfect — I'll shop there for my frozen perogies or a clay pot to grow some herbs on the balcony. I was forgetting that this wasn't my life.

I did have a life of my own. A full one in Calgary with my own work projects, including a new novel, that were being pushed aside. Whole paragraphs would sing out to me at unpredictable moments as I wandered Vancouver only to be left unrecorded. There was also a husband not used to captaining the ship solo, and Cole, Hudson, and Lily in various stages of needing my attention. When I found myself wearing Zoë's denim jacket and contemplating whether to buy the girls the plum or aqua placemats in the tidy home décor shop beside the best-ever cinnamon bun joint, I gave myself a shake. Students don't have friggin' placemats; they eat off pizza boxes. And I needed to break my cinnamon bun habit.

A Toronto friend told me there was a new term for releasing a child from the nest called *launching*. Launching sounded far too fast to me — like a rocket ship zooming into the vast unknown. I was attempting a slow-release program. But instead of easing Zoë out, I was easing back down memory lane. Pinching myself, I remembered I graduated from my own university experience on the west coast, wearing six-inch shoulder pads, the same year DNA profiling was developed and Apple computers went on sale.

On my seventh and last day in Vancouver, I took Zoë and Anna to Jericho Beach and spouted off more motherly advice. "Hey, you two," I told them, pulling Zoë closer, "don't get so caught up with school work or partying that you forget to find your way back here or to Kits Beach. You have to appreciate that you're not on the prairie anymore — you know, come walk in the sand, fill your pockets with those tiny blue seashells. Stare out at the ocean." Both girls had their shoes off, despite the tepid fall day, and were making marks in the wet sand with their toes. Who knows if they were listening?

My other kids had been phoning from Calgary. Hudson wanted the toaster back, Cole had used up all the gas in the van, and Lily was arguing with her father about whether or not she was old enough to go to the mall alone (she was). It was time to let Zoë grow up and get back to nurturing the rest of my family — if buying gas counts as nurturing.

If ever I felt I needed to grab back time, it was the afternoon when Zoë and I stood on the sidewalk with the yellow cab — my ride to the airport — idling beside us. Zoë, unlike her little sister and me, isn't a crier; when she is sad, she tends to withdraw.

"Your life here will be the beginning of so much," I said, choking back tears. She hugged me hard and stiffened her narrow back.

"Thanksgiving is just five weeks away," I assured us both.

"Right," she said.

"Right," I said.

The taxi driver's English was poor, but no translation was needed for his murmurs of sympathy as he observed me from his rear-view mirror dabbing at my eyes as we traveled along the cherry tree–lined stretch of Marine Drive. I wiped sniffles into my jacket sleeve as my first child and I were separated by the wide Fraser River.

Pulling my suitcase down the long airport corridor, I wondered how Zoë was observing the beginning of her new freedom. I'd find out when she read about it on the radio. This time the hosts of the Vancouver CBC studio told her she was a natural, as she delivered her thoughts on her independence in her young, slightly sassy voice.

Man, the actual moving days flew by, though the process wasn't without a few kinks. The futon couch my auntie donated was not an easy thing to assemble, but Dad tackled the job with matchless vigor. Meanwhile, Mom and I both behaved like fifties housewives, arranging towels and blankets, and pots and pans whilst Father-dearest grunted and groaned in the background. Slowly but surely, my new home began to take shape.

In the whirlwind of putting everything together, I didn't have enough time for bon voyage bonding with my dad. After he left, I got to thinking about one night during our summer holidays. While we were watching a movie, Dad took my palm and began massaging it. He said, See, a hand massage can be just as comforting as any other massage. Then he stopped, probably thinking that sounded a little weird. I didn't really get it till later, when I realized he just needed a pretense for holding my hand. I wished I'd held on longer.

Anyway, the move went well, but somehow my parents managed to misplace two boxes of miscellaneous found objects that I wanted for art projects. I believe this is probably the work of my mother's mischievous feng shui gods, threatening my way of life with their repressing simplicity. On the other hand, we did bring the horrible toaster from home. The one that either barely heats or deeply burns anything inserted into it. I thought we'd left it behind, but, no, there it was in my apartment, still brimming with crumbs from the toasts of the past. Mom realized that if she gave me all the old household devices that plague her existence back home, she'd get to buy new things.

When the time for Mom's departure actually arrived, I helped her carry her luggage downstairs. Before she got into the cab, she told me, Be good, like she always does. We hugged again and I felt her start to cry, something I hadn't seen much of — yet. Caught off guard, I said right away, Don't cry, Mom. She tried to say, It's my party and I'll cry if I want to, but she stumbled over the words. I thanked her for helping me and said goodbye, and she said she'd probably see me sooner than I expected. No kidding. Then the cab pulled away and disappeared. I hooked my feet on a metal railing by the road and sat there for a while, just thinking.

I went back inside, pressed the button for the elevator, but changed my mind and took the stairs. As I walked up, I pressed on the tender areas of my neck and chest with the tips of my fingers, wondering why it always hurts in that same spot, right behind your throat, when you're sad but you can't cry. When I got to my floor, I stood still beside the door to the stairway going up to the roof. Anna and I had gone up there the first night we were left alone together to check out the view — the rolling streets that lead to the ferries and airport in one direction, glass high-rises of downtown in another, and off toward English Bay and the wide ocean down the hill.

I pushed open the door to the stairway to the roof and just kept ascending. How could I go home and cry when *home* had just got into a cab and left?

24

Chapter 5

It's Not Like I'm A Cry Baby Or Anything

Mom, I know better than to ignore your emails. If I ignore them, they start reproducing like rabbits. Sorry, I was busy.

– Email from Zoë

It's not like I'm a cry baby or anything. I'd say I'm an average crier. I kept it together for the final scene in the park in *You've Got Mail*, but when Tom Hanks gives Meg Ryan that daisy in her bedroom — oh boy. I held back tears in *Juno* when Juno and her dorky boyfriend made up in the school field, but I didn't stand a chance when they're in the maternity ward bed together after Juno gives birth to the baby they are giving up for adoption. Who wouldn't be overcome? Yet for months prior to Zoë leaving home, I would try to imagine her moving about in her own place and just thinking about it could bring me to tears. I don't know what it was that upset me — the vision of her alone in a quiet apartment or our noisy house without my oldest daughter's quiet presence. Once she was actually living in Vancouver, I seldom sniveled about it. Well, there was that one time I embarrassed Lily in front of the oh-so-together choir moms, but overall the waterworks didn't happen as often as I thought they would. Instead, the emotion I experienced from time to time on any given day was slow, simmering panic.

Ever since my four kids were little, I would get caught up in the pace of our day-to-day lives and forget about the concept of *parenting* as a verb. Then — out of the blue — a conversation with another, perhaps wiser, parent or a statement by a so-called *parenting expert* would give me pause. I would get reflective and analytical about some of our more disgraceful family habits or our collective psychological well-being. Off I would tear to the bookstore to read up and re-evaluate my techniques, bringing home tomes as strategic as *101 Ways to Help Your Daughter Love Her Body* or as touchy-feely as *The Optimistic Child.*

The supper table had always been the preeminent place to get at least the feigned attention of my teenagers and address any parenting oversights. The year before Zoë left, the book that had captured my attention was *365 Manners Kids Should Know*. The book follows a calendar, each day addressing a new manner. Clearly, the author had never studied the attention spans of my children. My strategy was to fly through ten or twenty manners in a sitting, adopting the same supersonic speed as their favourite shoot 'em up video game or a MuchMusic countdown. I summarized the highlights for them. "Okay, it says here you can actually eat asparagus with your fingers." Unfortunately, three of my four children wouldn't swallow a piece of asparagus no matter what appendage they were using to pick it up. "And it says it's rude to blow on your food." The author had obviously never been late for piano lessons.

My youngest son, Hudson, always searching for a contrary angle, grabbed the book and ran his hand pensively over his new buzz cut. "Are you sure you want this lady to be our manner guru, Mom? She says right here that it's rude to be late for *anything*." I gave up, tossing the book aside, which is why Zoë left home with only enough manners to get her into late March.

She was, in effect, missing nine months of manners. My other staple books addressed the relationship between mothers and daughters (of course, I also had been known to peruse ones especially for *mothers and sons*). The author of the last mother/daughter book I read went for the jugular. She talked about how this stage in a mother's life was especially difficult, because while my daughter was blossoming and truly coming into her own, my blossoming had peaked decades ago and I was now on a downward stretch. Maybe she didn't put it quite so bleakly, but that was clearly what she meant.

The sentiment shared by some of my closest friends was that I should be calm through all of these changes, that Zoë moving out was a natural phenomenon — a healthy, normal part of the cycle of life. Of course, these well-meaning women all happened to be the parents of younger children. They were still reading *How to Talk So Your Children Will Listen* and believed that feat was achievable. My friends with teens recognized that the book should have been called *How to Scream Really, Really Loudly So That Your Children Believe Something Has Gone Terribly Wrong and Might Listen.*

It was from this latter group that I received a tantalizing idea. When two of these seasoned mothers heard that Zoë was living in her own apartment, they both recommended video cams — one on my computer and one on Zoë's. I assumed they were joking. Why in the world would I want to spy on my daughter? I thought at first.

But the more I thought about it, the better I liked the idea.

I didn't care if she was eating her asparagus with her fingers. But once she had been on her own for a while, there was a whole lot of other information I wanted to gather. Did she eat a green vegetable ever? I was hoping for a few peas or a chunk of broccoli, maybe a bit of lettuce squished into her sandwich. Was salsa her veggie of choice?

What else would a video cam reveal? Would I see her emptying her pockets of seashells from the beachcombing excursion I had implored her to take as a break from school, or would she pull out one of those art school *roll-your-own* cigarettes? I had left a brand new mini-vacuum cleaner still in its box at her front door. Would the camera reveal Zoë and Anna using the box as a hallway table for keys and books? Speaking of keys — she was locking the door behind her every single time like I insisted, wasn't she? At what late hour would the camera record her coming in? Would she look tired and weary? She's a girl who keeps odd hours, but unlike her sister, Lily, who runs like a Duracell battery, Zoë has always needed her sleep. What about that leftover sushi? Was it still in the refrigerator from my stay weeks ago? A carload of friends had already made the trip to visit her from Calgary. She had been over the moon with enthusiasm, eager to tour them through her school and take them across the inlet to downtown on one of the rainbow-coloured ferry boats, stopping for buck-a-slice pizza, before returning to the west side by walking across the Granville Street Bridge. But did she muck out the bathtub before they arrived and put out clean towels? Was she a good host to her peeps? I don't think hosting was covered in the first three months of our manners guide.

I had so many questions that a video cam could answer, but what did I really want to know? If we had invested in the video cam, I would have told her, "Put your face up close to the camera. Closer, Zoë. I want to see if you're happy or sad or homesick. I want to see if you need me."

We didn't get a video cam, but despite my inability to be an electronic bug on the wall of Zoë's apartment, we were learning to communicate through alternate means. When Lily left home, we had instant texting, but with Zoë, it was an email relationship we had to develop. She sent us missives, sharing when she was lonely or missing her boyfriend and us. I'd send her back cheery emails from home, just like the letters my mom sent to me by Canada Post in the eighties. Those took five days to arrive. So why did it drive me to distraction when I had to wait for Zoë to respond to my heartfelt messages after they bleeped their way in mere seconds across an entire mountain range and an alpine valley, to the coast? Unlike me and my mother, who, of course, considered long-distance calls an extravagance when I started university in Toronto in 1979, Zoë and I spoke on the phone a few times a week, but in between, I was bound to remember an urgent question or something I absolutely *had* to let her know. I wanted a quick response, but, no, she would make me wait — sometimes six or seven hours. When she finally did answer to tell me sorry but she hadn't had time to rent the movie *The Royal Tenenbaums* as per my recommendation or to fill out her Christmas wish list, she would also inform me that she was so swamped with art projects that she was now taking time away from her personal hygiene and nutritional needs to respond to my *threats*. Come on — I wouldn't really have stopped paying her rent. All I wanted was a teeny email.

Zoë had her moments, too. One evening in late autumn, she called just as I was shutting the house down for the night. "Mom, you heard about all those people taken hostage in Russia, at that theatre?"

"I did, Zoë."

"They just wanted to see a musical and now they're captives. It's so freaky."

"It's awful."

"I'm so lonely, Mom."

"Ah, honey," I said. "Where's Anna tonight?"

"In her room doing homework. But I'm lonely for you guys. What's everyone there doing?"

"Let's see," I said, trying to decide if our activities would make her more or less melancholy, "Cole was complaining about his math and trying to decide if he should get a buzz cut like Hudson's. Hudson said he didn't care what Cole did because he was growing his hair back, and went downstairs to play the guitar. I reminded Cole that a buzz cut will show the scars on his skull from all the stitches he had as a little kid. He said scars are cool and went to bed. Dad was watching *The Graduate* again. But he just went to bed, too."

"I love *The Graduate*. I wish I was watching it with him."

"I'll tell Dad that."

"Was Cole doing algebraic expressions? I hated that unit. You should tell Hud to call me sometime. What about Lily? How's Lily?"

"You know — Lily-ish. She's worried that a certain girlfriend doesn't like her again. I'm glad you two talk. She misses you."

It was tough for thirteen-year-old Lily, Will, and me to have Zoë away, but we squeezed every second out of our long-distance telephone plan. Her brothers, Cole and Hudson, weren't phone-talkers and hardly spoke to her at all. I worried that my children could drift apart.

Zoë was in Vancouver for two long months before coming home for a weekend in November. One of the final pieces that she shared with the CBC Radio audience aired just before we were reunited with her that autumn.

Right now, I'm in another crunch period, preparing to go home for the long weekend. Last night, I was at school till eleven working on a colour class assignment focused on the many different shades of gray in the universe. It put me in a rather melancholy mood. By the time I got back to the apartment, I was feeling awfully homesick. I was going to call home, but I didn't feel like dealing with my mom's accusations of infrequent emails. Calling as much as she'd like is hard. She doesn't understand that between Anna and I and our respective boyfriends in two different prairie provinces, coordinating phone time is difficult as it is.

So instead of calling, I decided to occupy myself by putting up the red twinkly lights I used to have in my bedroom back home. But while I was working, I found one crocheted finger-piece from a glove my friend Joy had been making when she came out to visit, and suddenly I missed everyone in Calgary so much I thought I was going to break down and cry. I grabbed the phone and dialed up Mom. After all, no one sleeps in my house before midnight.

I asked how things were, lay back on my bed, and let myself get lost in the family details. Hudson's girlfriend picked up and went to Berlin for three weeks. Lily made it into the Cantaré choir opera. Cole busted up his hand on the rails at the high school. When finally I had to hang up and get some sleep, I tucked myself in beneath the glow of red twinkle lights and tapped my ankles together three times. There's no place like home. There's no place like home. There's no place like home.

And so we had Zoë with us for her short fall reading break. On the Friday and Saturday nights, the house filled up with family and three or four of her best friends. But Sunday, close to dusk, each of my four kids trickled back home from separate outings. From upstairs, I could hear them talking softly in the living room. Coming down, I found them in the dark — the boys showing their affection for their sisters in their odd boy way. They had dog piled on Zoë and Lily. It was reassuring to witness them that way, like a big pile of puppies heaped on top of each other.

One of my few friends with children older than mine had warned me that Zoë would have changed. "I know it hasn't been long," she said, "but, trust me, she'll be different, more grown-up. You'll see." I had been nervous. I didn't want her to change, or even grow up particularly. I would still rather have spent my evenings driving her to piano lessons or to her girlfriends' houses, instead of emailing her in Vancouver or fighting for phone time with her long distance boyfriend. But my friend was right. My eldest daughter was different. She hadn't undergone a total epiphany or anything. She didn't say, "Mommy, I've realized how burdened you've been looking after us four kids. Put your feet up and let me vacuum up the nacho crumbs before I massage your tired shoulders."

But she *was* different. I noticed it the first evening she was back as we lingered around the table after dinner, bombarding her with questions. It was a look on her face, a quality it was hard to put my finger on, except to say that she *had* drifted away a little bit. I had gazed around the room at the others, Cole and Hudson and Lily, and imagined us all reuniting after future ventures. Zoë swore that she would travel to the far north someday, captivated by the notion of visiting Yellowknife or even Inuvik, whereas Cole insisted he was going to snowboard in the southern hemisphere in Queenstown, New Zealand. Hudson was harder to pin down — I think he aspired to travel back and forth in time — and back then I wrongly viewed Lily as a homebody. I wanted my kids to have fabulous adventures, but for the upcoming Christmas season, I was happy imagining them all staying put. For the three weeks that Zoë would be home, I was going to pretend that she had never left. We would decorate a too-tall, slightly lopsided tree together, and Will would insist, once more, on crowning it with the pissed-off looking angel Zoë made in kindergarten. I imagined my kids dog piling on top of one another and watching Bing Crosby's *White Christmas*. As always, Will's sisters would cap off the big family Christmas Eve party singing the Sister's song about sticking together.

I intended to encourage Zoë to humour Lily and me, and come skating with us on the lake near their grandparent's property. After that, we would go for steamers, before coming home to whip up a batch of date-filled butter tarts for Christmas Eve, filling the house with the aroma of toasting brown sugar. She'd be impatient to hang out with her friends (who would happily devour the butter tarts), but I hoped I could convince her to indulge us with a skate around the lake first. I'd ask, but I promised myself to be a grown-up about it and not harass her — just ask. At ages eighteen and thirteen, my daughters were in different stages of their lives, but I knew that on Christmas Eve they would raise their voices and happily sing together.

Some people say girls are easier than boys. "Oh, no, no, no," others will tell you, "boys are easier." I'm not sure what exactly *easier* encompasses. Easier to get along with? Easier to discipline? Easier to lose your mind worrying over? I do know that when Zoë went off to study art at Emily Carr, I thought a mother must only feel this out of sorts once. But a year later, I had to *launch*, as they say in those swishy mother circles, her exuberant brother, Cole. Kids being kids, no two alike and all that, there was hardly an ounce of knowledge I could borrow from Zoë leaving when Cole decided to follow suit...

Chapter 6

Snowboard Boy's First Suit

Be careless in your dress if you will, but keep a tidy soul.

– Mark Twain

Considering what we'd paid to turn Zoë into the belle of the ball at graduation, when it was Cole's turn, his dad and I graciously decided to upgrade his wardrobe of scrubby jeans, t-shirts, and hoodies, and buy him a suit, instead of going the rented tux route. One of Cole's crew informed me that the rental shop *he'd* gone to had offered him insurance in case he threw up on his tux, i.e. *a barf policy*, and I momentarily rethought suit shopping. Zoë had made sketches and designed her own glam outfit. I believe Cole only went along with getting dressed up because the store I suggested was at the mall and he was looking forward to a double cheeseburger with bacon from the food court. His buddy came along, also more enthused over the promised burger than the main objective of our shopping trip.

The absolutely most dressed up Cole had been in his seventeen years was cords, new runners, and perhaps a tucked-in shirt for half an hour. "Even if you don't wear the jacket often, it'll be nice to have dress pants," I reasoned, as we deliberated between the not-too-cheap and the not-cheap-at-all suits. "Sure," Cole said, slipping into a herringbone jacket while the salesperson, who was barely older than my son, calculated his size. Then Cole tripped me up by asking, "Dress pants for what though?"

"Well, you know, you don't know what your plans are for next year. You might get a job where you need something special." All three boys — my son, his friend, and the young sales guy — considered Cole's image in the mirror: the classic jacket over his Billabong t-shirt and baggy jeans, with his baseball cap tipped backwards. They all turned to me, waiting for further explanation.

"For instance, you might sell suits," was all that sprang to mind.

"Sure," Cole answered skeptically. He'd applied to a few universities but was leaning heavily toward taking a *gap year* — newly named in our part of the world. His most recent employment aspiration was to work as a snowboard instructor; the further from home the mountains, the better. The last time I checked snowboard instructors weren't wearing suits.

Attempting to get us back on task, the young sales guy asked Cole if he'd like to try the pants on. Not understanding that it was a rhetorical question, Cole said, "Nah, I'll just take them." Shopping, or any other slow-paced activity, had never been his forte. As a baby, being held was too sedentary for him. He grew into a kid who, when he wasn't playing sports, was calling friends up to *skate some rails*. His greatest achievement in the eyes of me and his father, the two people he depended on to deliver him to the clinic for stitches to his head or casts for his broken bones, was that he sat still for some six hours a day in a classroom for twelve long years. His studies, at which he'd nevertheless managed to succeed, were an exercise in halting perpetual motion.

The sales guy tried again, suggesting Cole try on both pieces with a proper shirt. "I'll probably just wear one of my dad's,"

Cole said, and I pictured him in kindergarten wearing an old dress shirt of his father's buttoned up backwards to keep the fingerpaint off. The sight I was treated to a few minutes later was stunning: my seventeen-year-old kid all put together in a gray herringbone suit. Sock footed, but otherwise put together. All three of us stared at Cole, who stared at himself in the mirror. "Dude, it makes you look older," his friend said.

"Yeah, you're not kidding," Cole agreed.

I swallowed. The sales guy had seen blubbering mothers before. He turned away to give us our moment of awe. The suit didn't make Cole appear older to me. It made him look handsome, but not *older*. In fact, I couldn't get the image of him in kindergarten out of my mind, which was making me come undone. When did Cole go from wearing his dad's shirt that trailed on the paint-spattered floor to it almost fitting him?

We found him a shirt of his own, ordered minor alterations to the suit, and paid up, before heading off to get the boys their burgers. They choked them down while scoping out teenage girls in the food court, oblivious to me getting out a pen and paper and trying to gather my thoughts. I'd dealt with Zoë leaving home to attend art school. She had returned for summer break, refusing my request to wear a surgical mask on the plane because of the SARS epidemic. She was lifeguarding at the local pool for the summer and had invited me down for a swim, promising that no harm would come to me on her watch. It struck me as a funny reversal. No one watching my uneven front crawl would have believed I was more concerned about the lifeguard than she was about me.

But what about this boy? The son I had to remind that we, his parents, were in fact sometimes in charge? Was he equipped to survive away from *moi*? Once again, I had to tally up what my teenaged kid did and didn't know before he forged his own path into the great unknown.

My kids had all mastered food foraging. Judging from the theme he'd chosen for his bedroom — monk-like austerity — I didn't have to worry that he would get lost in a mishmash of belongings the way his older sister and younger brother could. This amazing son would even gather up those clothes from time to time and do laundry, which was one of his most admirable characteristics.

Cole interrupted my reverie to ask if I'd mind if they went off on their own for a few minutes to get the phone number of a girl they'd never laid eyes on until five minutes before. "And you think she'll give it to you?" I asked incredulously.

"Sure. Why wouldn't she?"

Optimism would get him places. "Stalk her politely, then," I said, before ducking out of sight to make some quick notations.

Did he know how to handle money? (He was an expert at getting me to hand it over, if that counted.) Could he change a tire? (Could I?) Would he trust the right people? (Should he be wary of strange girls in the mall? Or perhaps just their boyfriends and parents?)

My anxiety was intensifying. Had I told him you can't turn right on a red light in some cities? To disinfect all his cuts? How to recognize a rabid animal? To leave a window open in a tornado?

My pen couldn't keep up. I switched to a sloppy shorthand. What about girls? Did I ever explain to him that they honestly just wanted him to listen, not to solve their problems?

"Are you okay, Mom?" he asked, catching up with me. "You have your worried look on."

"I'm fine. Let's get you some shoes."

"Sure. Whatever. But not tonight, okay? We're meeting some guys for basketball behind the school, but thanks for the cool suit, Mom."

"Whatever," I said nonchalantly. "Did that girl give you her number?"

"Nah, her mom showed up."

It was refreshing and filled me with optimism to see my oldest son all decked out in that new herringbone suit, but it was this Cole who I wanted to spend more time with — the one in jeans and a baseball cap, planning a game of three-on-three basketball and dodging girls' moms in the mall.

Chapter 7

Gap or Gorge?

Go then if you must, but remember, no matter how foolish your deeds, those who love you will love you still.

– *Sophocles,* Antigone

After having to cajole and sweet talk Cole, Hudson, and Lily into beginning a university education, I have come out strongly in favour of, as the Brits say, *the gap year*. I first heard the term in a newspaper article about Prince William who was taking a year off between completing his high school *A-levels* and beginning his studies at Scotland's prestigious St. Andrews University. Prince William was going to spend this year working on a UK farm, teaching English in a remote part of Chile, hunting on an African safari, and trekking in Belize with the Welsh Guards. My son's plans weren't so lofty, but he too was about to embark on a *gap year*.

When Zoë was eight years old, I allowed her to choose from a list of after-school programs at the community centre. She wanted me to sign her up for art lessons. "Come on, Zoë, pick something else," I remember saying. "You do art on your own all the time.

What about gymnastics or maybe basketball with Cole?" She finally chose Highland dancing and hated every jump over the imaginary sword. All Zoë ever wanted was to study art and so she sailed from grade twelve to art school with nary a moment of existential angst. This wasn't the case with Cole. Cole's plans for the near future were vague and nerve-racking.

I like the term *gap year* and I'm drawn to the definition for *gap* in Webster's dictionary — *a break in continuity*. Like many parents who had to encourage and push their reluctant or extremely energetic kids through twelve years of school, we verbalized our support for Cole taking a gap year in hopes that it would lead him to decide all on his own, and with *conviction*, "I want to go back to school. I clearly see the benefit of continuing my education." Of course, this effect is best achieved if working hard at a low-paying job, but not spending too much money or time in pubs and clubs, crowd-surfing in mosh pits, or drunk with freedom from math homework and biology pop quizzes.

Like mother, like son, was how I thought of it. My own father had feared the gap year. I graduated in 1977 from the same high school that Cole attended. Will and I had bought the spacious house that I grew up in from my parents the year after Lily was born, so certain aspects of my life mirrored my kids'. When I should have been studying for my grade twelve math final exam, I had been stretched across my girlfriend's bed listening to Elton John belt out "Goodbye Yellow Brick Road" and daydreaming about visiting Paris, Rome, and Barcelona as soon as our summer jobs had earned us enough to purchase airfare, a youth hostel card, a Eurail pass, an awkward, heavy backpack, and the requisite pair of hiking boots. When I informed *my* dad that my departure would be at the same time university classes were beginning, he made a desperate bid to fund a portion of my trip if only I could squeeze it into the summer months. I refused, wanting nothing more than for time to stretch out ahead of me. I began my adventure trekking through drizzling rain to the original village of Calgary on the island of Mull in Scotland, the place Colonel Macleod of the North West Mounted Police had chosen as our Canadian city's namesake. My girlfriend and I found the tiny village from which the famous Colonel originated and knocked on the door of a stranger's house. We were invited in for a tiny glass of the most mellow, smoky Scotch by one of the Colonel's sexy young male descendants. Had my mother been able to receive a text or email, she would certainly have discouraged our plan. Hearing the tale after the fact, she was proud of our audacity.

Flying across the Atlantic ocean, I had left the shelter of my parent's house where not only was there meat and potatoes on the table every evening at six, but my siblings and I had the luxury of driving ourselves around in my dad's Chrysler LeBaron. Crisscrossing Europe, I learned to stretch my limited food budget in costly delis and pastry shops, and struggled to decipher train schedules in several languages, all with little communication with anyone back home. So, of course, I was in support of Cole taking a year off with a plan to save money for some sort of maturing adventure — maybe not an African safari like Prince Will but perhaps a journey similar to mine. When I travelled in the seventies, phone calls home seemed astronomically expensive. Looking back, I wonder if they really were beyond my parents' means or if everyone was simply accustomed to being out of touch. I would remind myself that Cole's aim was to *leave home behind*, just like mine had been decades earlier.

His first goal was to earn the cash he'd need. In a perverse way, we were happy to see him slugging it out as an underpaid *landscaper*, which amounted to nothing more than long days of shoveling soil and hauling sidewalk blocks. When he started, he'd come home with dirt under his nails and up his nose and ask me, "Can you believe they work more than a forty-hour week? Who works more than forty hours a week?" Autumn's frost came typically early, and when that job ended, he signed on with a firm that installed furnaces and heating ducts. But he had itchy feet. Like multitudes of Canadian (and Australian) kids, his real dream was to spend a winter at a ski resort with a job on, or anywhere near, a mountain, living like a bohemian. We were shakily okay with that plan. Shortly before his exodus, he arrived home from being out the entire night, and, good kid that he was, politely asked that I look at the back of his head. "Aw, gross," I said, parting the sticky hair and seeing that his bloody skull had a split in it that should have been stitched hours ago. He had interrupted me talking on the phone to Zoë, who'd just informed me that she was lying on the floor of her Vancouver apartment, listening to the pouring rain and trying (in a melancholy mood) to comprehend the meaning of life. I wanted to quote *The Prophet* to her, but instead we both listened to her brother provide details of his moshing accident.

A university campus might have been a safer environment for the exploits of a not-quite-eighteen-year-old boy, but he was intent on snowboarding through the winter with a pack of other bohemian wannabes. (Three of my four kids graduated high school six months shy of being eighteen. Warning: when thinking your chatty, smart four-year-old is ready to start school, consider whether you want him to be the youngest of his friends drinking, swearing, and asserting himself as a teenager in grade ten.)

While a few of Cole's friends were still saving hard to travel to Thailand or Australia, Cole felt suitably wealthy with nine hundred dollars in his bank account to set out for Whistler Blackcomb Resort in British Columbia and make his mark on the snowboarding world. Strangely, our kids never went to camp as youngsters. Maybe our grassy backyard in the summer with a half dozen of their friends *was* camp enough for them. So, as Cole turned on *The Simpsons* and spread his gear out in the TV room the night before he was to leave, he was packing to go away from home for the first time without family (at least for longer than his three-day high school campout). He insisted that he wasn't going to bring much, but by the time he had enough jeans and t-shirts, all his snowboarding gear, heavy socks, and favourite hoodies, as well as his books and CDs, hacky sacks, and shaving kit, he had to switch from a backpack to a big duffle. With his room empty of his most desired belongings and the duffle full, he sat on his floor programming his new phone with a pensive look on his face.

"Do you feel kinda funny?" I asked him.

"Shit, Mom, yeah. But I don't know why. I'm so ready to do this."

I told him that his grandpa had explained it to me years ago with an analogy. We all have dens where we've matted down the grass and we're comfortable. Now Cole was leaving his den and he didn't have a new one yet, or even know where it would be. (He'd learned that the challenge wasn't so much finding a job in Whistler than finding affordable accommodation.) I told him Grandpa's theory was that until he got comfortable in a new den and got the grass matted down there, he might feel unsettled.

"Hell, yeah," he said. "That's good, Mom. Yeah, I get that."

So it was under a blue sky on a November day that his dad and I drove Cole to the airport to get on a plane to Vancouver. From there, he and his buddy, Hugo, would bus to the wilds of Whistler, BC. Now *I* know Whistler Blackcomb is a nice resort, but I was just as aware that my son and Hugo would be mixing with the less aristocratic side of town, a whole cacophony of wanderlust-struck teenagers. In the desperate days before he left, I tried to introduce him to a new hobby to while away the hours off the slopes so he didn't fall victim to a life of partying, but the kid didn't want to try his hand at calligraphy or learn to speak Japanese or Swahili with Berlitz language CDs. He was bringing his guitar and new books on Buddhism. Oh, and I had insisted on getting him a cellphone — for my needs, not his.

It was my second time through having a kid leave home and I thought I was getting better at keeping my emotions in check, but the WestJet airline agent quickly pushed me over the edge. Cole and Hugo had taken their mothers' advice and shaved before their job interviews. Seeing their fresh faces over their duffels, snowboards, sleeping bags, and the guitar, the agent must have guessed that they weren't seasoned travellers. He explained in a respectful but detailed way the gate location, baggage tags, and boarding time, as if he knew that, although the boys were attempting to appear casual, they were having trouble concentrating. I blinked and blinked, but still choked up. The WestJet guy didn't help by saying, "Oh no, here come the waterworks from Mom." Cole responded by giving me and his dad a big tight hug, and Hugo said he would hug us, too, if his hands weren't full. It's not that I didn't want them to grow up. Growing up is okay, but watching my second child heading toward airport security didn't make me feel *secure* at all.

Travelling home from the airport on the snowy road at seven in the morning, both Will and I were feeling out of sorts. I cranked up the car's heat and thought about the enthusiastic hug Cole had given me and how he had never wanted to cuddle when he was little because he didn't want to be still for that long. In fact, he hadn't been very easy to pin down for the last few years either, in between part-time jobs and school. He did his homework when he should have been sleeping, cramming for an algebra exam or typing his English essay on *True Blood* in the hours before sunrise. Late at night, he slipped in and out of the house to snowboard, performing rails on precarious outdoor stairways, or, in warmer weather, he would longboard steep roads at three a.m., despite being ratted out by alarmed siblings and threatened by me.

As we turned onto the freeway from the airport, Will said pragmatic things like "It'll be good for him," and "They all have to move out sooner or later." Met with my silence, he turned on the radio and added, "This is the only way they grow up." Still, I was stunned by how fast it had happened. When he was a toddler, Cole had these wild blond curls. When they started to fall over the collar of his little t-shirts, I took him to a barber for a trim, but annoyingly the man ignored my directions and cut his lovely locks off before I could stop him. The summer before he left home, Cole had eschewed the popular buzz cut style and grown his hair out for an edgier snowboard-guy look. I hadn't let on how thrilled I was to see the return of his only slightly darker curls. However, Whistler Blackcomb had an extensive grooming policy on their potential employee website, specifying *mid-ear and above the collar* hair length. To comply with the regulations, Cole left with his new curls snipped off again.

Will and I made it home, and I made cinnamon apple pancakes for the two teens still residing there, fifteen-year-old Hudson and thirteen-year-old Lily (though I had to shake them awake to get them up to eat). Then I straightened the mess Cole had left after I suggested he lighten the load in his over-stuffed duffel.

I had launched another kid. Cole was now looking for a den, and I was back to being that mother bear. I was going to lumber about in circles for a week or two, bewildered and confused, clinging to my cellphone and the two younger kids left at home.

Whistler Blackcomb Resort held its hiring fair in November but warned potential staff that they wouldn't actually be working until there was sufficient snow. After spending his nine hundred bucks waiting for that to happen, Cole found himself with the highly sought-after position of *liftie,* or, as he stated in subsequent resumes, he was *responsible for the safety and operation of the fastest upload capacity lift in North America.* Two weeks shy of his eighteenth birthday, he had landed his dream job. He was able to snowboard from the small apartment in staff housing which he shared with two strangers from Quebec to the chairlift that would take him to his station at the top of the mountain. He was so high up that he actually had cell service — there was nothing to interfere with the signal up there — and he would occasionally call me before the first skiers showed up. "Mom, it's sweet up here. The sky is pink, seriously pink, and I can see over half a dozen mountains. It's dope."

"Should you be on your phone?"

"My shift hasn't started. It's weird when there's no one coming up the lift. Kinda ... I dunno ... lonely. I mean, it's just me up here."

Cole called often in the beginning, justifying his need for contact by making requests. Could I send him some contact solution, he'd ask: "You wouldn't believe how they rip you off here." The next day, it would be an appeal for the super warm gloves they sell in outdoor supply stores. I tried to explain that the cost of sending them outweighed the savings, but then he told me all the kids from Quebec were getting care packages from home. Mother guilt worked on me like a charm, and I had Lily help me make up a care package — a new hackie sack, some macho aftershave, vitamin C and D, Jon Krakauer's latest book, and Cole's favourite (expensive) energy bars, all packed tightly around the gloves and contact solution. Other times, he would call and ask to speak to Hudson, and, eavesdropping, I realized he was sharing the wilder aspects of being a liftie that I wasn't privy to. As he made new friends, his cell service became less *reliable*. I'd interrupt him at the snowboard park trying to execute *seven-twenties*, his friends hollering in the background, or at a party any night of the week, a rapper rhyming nearby. "Sorry, Mom, I think I'm losing you," he'd shout.

"I just wanted to see how you're doing, Cole," I'd shout back. "Do you have a cold? It sounds like you have a cold. Take that vitamin D. You know what they say about vitamin D."

"Everything's cool, Mom. You're breaking up," he'd say, and I was supposed to believe he was out of cell range when he *lost* me.

Recently, I asked Cole what it was like leaving home for the first time for that iconic Canadian winter job. Aware that Zoë had shared her perspective on the CBC, Cole said he would surprise me with his point of view, and I found this short essay on my desk.

Something my mother never knew was that my decision to leave Calgary was mostly about putting distance between me and a girl. In fact, most of my decisions in the last decade have been about women... I was seventeen and never wanted my parents to know much about me at that age. I interpreted every attempt they made to be conversational and genuinely curious about my life as an attempt to hold on. My parents had no idea that taking the opportunity to head to Whistler, BC, came about because I was escaping from the possibility of a relationship. I had a new girlfriend, and for an anxious day or two, she thought she might be pregnant, despite our nervously taking every precaution we'd learned in our fleeting Sex Ed class taught by an equally nervous teacher. She never was pregnant to both of our mind-numbing reliefs, but she did want to "have a relationship." The whole episode had shown me how clearly I wasn't ready for that, and, having stayed until the fact of her non-pregnancy was undoubtedly proven, I made plans to exit.

That all sounds harsher than it was. I was so naive, it's almost laughable. My naivety was due to the fact that I was a pretty overweight kid until seventeen when I lost, like, twenty pounds, and the thought of kissing a girl was unexpectedly a reality. I lost my virginity, made friends with the cool kids, and started going to parties all in the span of six months. I can't even take credit for my sudden social status; one of my new "friends" thought it was a novelty to prance around with the goofy-nerd-who-now-suddenly-has-strong-features. It was him and his "cool" friend who wanted to get me drunk and watch as I embarrassingly announced my undying love for just about every girl I met. I was the good kid and had gotten great grades so I felt I deserved some of this new fun. After maybe six months of this, I realized that my friend was no longer challenging me and, in a lot of ways, was using me for his own amusement. The situation with the girl came about suddenly — basically, she was my first ever girlfriend. But the brief parenthood scare made me realize that we hardly knew each other, and not wanting to be a couple, I carried on with my plan to leave.

For me, that first time I left home wasn't a gap year, a phrase that implies that I might have known what it was a break between; rather, it was an attempt at coming of age. I wanted to be an adult, date a real woman, and get involved in some kind of intellectual scene. I can't believe I thought all those things would happen in Whistler.

I landed in a staff housing unit with hundreds of young people much like me, getting away from something or trying to find something, but they were mostly dudes and I was the youngest of everyone. Some of the guys liked to get into fights, and I was definitely not into that. And to top it off, many of them did drugs to compensate for the lack of babes in the area. I drank beer but never had experiences with real drugs — cocaine or ecstasy — and I didn't want my first drug experience to be with a bunch of sweaty guys in a stinky building. I was still seventeen at the time, and no way was I about to sacrifice my first time doing anything in a building so crappy that one day a friend of mine "dropped" a pizza down a stairwell and there was pepperoni stuck to the walls from that day until the day I moved out.

I turned to snowboarding. Becoming the outdoors guy was not exactly what I set out to do, but it seemed like a viable option. Some of the other guys had jobs in the kitchen, serving greasy food. Not me. I got a job supervising the lift at the very top of Whistler Mountain, which came with enormous perks. Have you seen Whistler? It's the tallest ski hill in North America. And I had only four days of work instead of five per week. Occasionally I had the otherworldly experience of riding a snowmobile in the dark up to the highest run, the machine's light bouncing off the snow in the still predawn. In those four months, I was able to snowboard one hundred and twenty days *in a row*. In the face of all that snowboarding, the rush to meet women and become an adult had faded once again. Now I was an adrenaline junkie. So how did my mom fit into this?

Consciously, I had few thoughts of her, but my parents created an atmosphere of safety and support. If anything happened, I could always go back home, and I knew that. When I did return home, I was on a new path. I had decided I wanted to be a professional snowboarder. My thoughts of growing up were still immature, and it was the thrill that I was chasing. Women were a huge setback for me in terms of Whistler and the next year it would be even worse. Nonetheless, I have heard horror story after horror story of sex and STDs in the mountain village, and I'm happy to announce a clean bill of health in that department. And if we were to talk about Freud, I think it would be fair to say that my mother has given me high hopes for trying to find a wonderful woman so that, wherever I go, I never engage with low-hanging fruit.

As Cole would tell me, as the winter carried on, working alone at the top of the mountain got lonelier, and the nights, in contrast, were chaotic and laden with an excess of cannabis. Cole came home in the early spring determined to save up for one more adventure. His job, bussing tables at a popular bar on what would become Calgary's famous Red Mile, was cut short by an Easter snowboard accident that left him with a cast on his arm and time to contemplate his new fascination with Buddhism. He had the itch to further his travels and suddenly ached to return to the freedom he'd known on the slopes of Whistler Blackcomb, which, while not Prince William's Belize or remote Chile, represented a mecca of sorts for him. It was there he'd first taken care of himself while living in a community of young people, even if he was isolated by his age. For a snowboard season, he'd escaped the confines of our rules, forged his way in the world, and learned to make a decent bean and rice wrap.

Nevertheless, with his one good hand, he typed up an application to university, not St. Andrews in Scotland, but a fine university in Calgary. We held our breaths. He talked more of Whistler, of the power of sunrises over the peaks, of friendships forged. *Forward,* we whispered in his ear. "Talk to your big sister, Zoë. Zoë loves being a student again." (Of course, Zoë always liked being a student.) "Try university. Study whatever you think you'd like. The boy/girl ratio is two to three." (We were crafty.) "You did Whistler. You worked. You broke your arm."

He was accepted. He laid an old sleeping bag out in the backyard on a hot summer's day and chose courses — an eclectic array of mind-expanding areas of study. Still he wondered whether he shouldn't take more time off, make the gap larger, let it turn into a chasm, an abyss, a gorge...

Cole attended a university orientation for three days in early September, leaving the house for the C-Train freshly showered, perhaps shaved (it was hard to tell), but grumbling, "This thing will be lame. Shit like this is always lame." Returning late that first afternoon, he had changed his tune. The way he went on to Hudson, who was beginning grade eleven, about the kids he knew and the *tight* barbecue and how he got on stage at some point to address his peers, you'd have thought I'd slipped him twenty bucks to encourage Hudson to go to university.

It seemed fitting to offer Cole (who would start in general studies and switch to film production) a ride on his first day. As we crossed the bridge high over Calgary's winding Bow River, I told him I was proud of him for making this decision. "I guess," he said, adjusting his hat. The look he seemed to have selected was *casual with a hint of mystic* — a 1940's style gangster hat, 1970's aviator glasses, his dad's plaid shirt from some other decade, his brother's jeans from this decade, and his own new running shoes.

We pulled into the campus bus loop behind a line of SUVs driven by this generation of hovering parents. I tried not to say too much. Cole gave me a high-five before grabbing his skateboard from the backseat and gliding away, asking directions from the first friendly-looking girl he spotted.

I let the car idle for a few minutes after he disappeared into the crowd of students. Hallelujah. We had made it through Cole's gap year. Too bad I couldn't remember what a positive experience the gap had been when it was Hudson's turn to strike out on his own.

Chapter 8

Twigs and Sticks and Bits of String

Your children are not your children...
You may house their bodies but not their souls,
For their souls dwell in the house of to-morrow,
which you cannot visit, not even in your dreams.

– Kahlil Gibran, The Prophet

An integral part of my strategy for dealing with an emptying nest was to help build new nests for my kids. When Zoë left home, I tried to mask my fear and insecurity by setting her up in her little apartment with every single *necessity* I could get my hands on. It was all so psychological — building that satellite nest, gathering symbolic twigs and sticks and bits of string. While she shyly made her way through the first days of classes, I had set out to an unfamiliar Ikea looking for whatever it was I hadn't thought of all summer in Calgary when I'd been pushing her to pack. "Get ready. Be prepared," was my motto during that time. It was advice

I often gave myself as I teared up at the thought of her no longer sitting at our dinner table.

Zoë had never even considered a gap year, but she was our first-born and a daughter — and I do buy into all that birth order pseudo-science. The gap had been *just* the ticket for Cole. I knew that to be absolutely true, so why did I hesitate to bring it up with Hudson? What fear makes us impatient parents so darn relieved to get our kids right back into school after one short summer between high school and post-secondary? It didn't have to be university. Will and I agreed that we would be supportive if our kids found their way into any sort of training toward developing a lucrative skill. True, they were all artistically inclined which came with its own job market challenges. We acted as if Hudson could lean either way, take a break or not, and — *la dee da* — we would be fine with his choice. But still we *encouraged* him to apply to various schools *just in case* he selected the option of starting one in the fall.

We all make parenting mistakes and, in time, forlornly recount them to others. What the heck was I thinking that summer when I stupidly *helped* seventeen-year-old Hudson apply to four post-secondary schools, all of whom accepted him, some with offers of scholarships? It's family lore now that when Hudson was a mere two years old and a quiet toddler who liked to cuddle, I pulled the evil trick on him of having another baby. Lily was jaundiced and always sleepy. During the evenings, I would get the other kids off to bed and make my own tired efforts to have alone time with the baby, who I felt I had neglected as she slept soundly in her bassinet all day. I still get emotional with sympathy for two-year-old Hudson when I remember my overwrought, but still insensitive, insistence that he stay in his bed (in a bedroom he shared with Cole so he wasn't really alone, I told my guilty self) while I held and nursed little Lily. That was the beginning of a fraught relationship between Lily and Hudson. Both have confessed to feeling jealous of the other receiving parental attention when they were young. It wasn't until Zoë and Cole were both living away from home that fifteen-year-old Hudson called a meeting with Lily in his bedroom. Sitting on Hudson's unmade bed, the two of them talked it out and determined that they needed to *have each other's backs* as the only kids in the house.

Hudson is a born philosopher. When his kindergarten teacher asked him what he wanted to be when he grew up, he said he wanted to see inside of people. "Like a doctor?" she asked. "No," Hudson said, staring at her through the lenses of his tiny wire-rimmed glasses. "No, I want to be really small and go see what it's like inside there." Cole once commented that while other kids got heavily into drugs in high school as an escape into an alternate reality, his brother Hudson got heavily into philosophy: Buddhism, Hinduism, Sufism, Taoism, Existentialism — all the -isms. There is no question he was a deep thinker, but he was just seventeen. What was I doing encouraging a seventeen-year-old boy to go off on his own to study? The poor kid couldn't say, "I'm too young to do this." Boys don't say things like that. Hovering be damned — that foresight should have been my area of expertise. I had long warned my friends not to let their kids start school at four-and-a-half-years-old. Now I also tell them not to send them off to university, especially boys, at just seventeen or eighteen. But no one, myself included, wants to heed that advice. We are all so anxious to have our kids take the next step. Proving what? I don't know. I should have clued in to Hudson's reluctance by how *impossibly* uninterested he had been in packing for his new life until the day before his departure.

The *launch* wasn't getting one bit easier for me. There was some comfort in Hudson having chosen the school Will and I attended, our alma mater, the University of Victoria, so he would be in a city and community we were familiar with. By the September that I drove Hudson out to Victoria, both Zoë and Cole had left home, though Cole's absence (four months at Whistler) had been brief compared to his sister's continuing education in Vancouver.

My relationships with my sons are so unlike those I have with my daughters. The boys resist my need to provide for them beyond the basic necessities of groceries and the use of my car. After my over-involvement in getting Hudson into university, I had tried to ease off pestering him — thank goodness, I didn't yet have the technology to text-stalk him. Delivering him to his dorm room in Victoria, British Columbia — a province, a mountain range, and a bit of ocean away from home — I came to grips with the idea that I was going to let another one go and promptly went into my let-me-replace-myself-with-fuzzy-blankets-and-the-right-supplies mode *again*.

Hudson had been the little guy who always lost his mittens and schoolbooks, the boy who couldn't keep track of his glasses and jean jacket, and the teen who was forever losing his wallet and cellphone. At seventeen, he had a deep voice and an angular, muscular frame, and was attempting to no longer involve me in the hunt for his misplaced belongings.

Hudson was patient with my hanging around town for a couple of days, but arriving on campus with a load of *necessities* from the mall, I hesitated at the stairway that led up to his dorm. "It's okay, Mom," he said. "None of these kids are clones. I'm not the only one with a mom wandering around here," though he insisted he would remake the bed with the new fleecy blanket himself.

On my last night in Victoria, I took him downtown to Pagliacci's, a favourite of Will and mine from back in the day, when we could only occasionally afford to eat out. Over bowls of creamy seafood pasta, Hudson and I talked in an easier manner than we had for some time. I then took the scenic drive along the ocean on the way back to the university, prolonging the moment when I would have to let go and overwhelmed with an urge to review parental lessons at a breakneck speed. Turning away from the water toward the campus, within a couple of blocks, I covered responsible drinking, meaningful relationships, and even safe sex. "They handed out condoms at orientation," he said. With that information, I chose to lighten up, though I was still searching for a *big* life motto, something he could tell Oprah was the truism his mother had imparted. How could I possibly be at a loss for words again?

The campus has a ring road circling it, but I knew the way to skirt behind the residence and avoid the long drive around. I took the ring road anyway, forcing my youngest son to linger with his mother who was so clearly on the verge of something dangerously emotional. As we drove around the ring, past those hallowed halls of education, we saw clusters of new students laughing and calling out to one another. All of Hudson's attention was, of course, directed outside the car. He was aching to reach for the cellphone in his pocket and connect with a female friend from home who was in Victoria, too. I appreciated his self-restraint.

"Don't be surprised if you get a low mark on your first paper. That happened to me a zillion years ago. I was shocked but I talked to the prof. You have to talk to the prof."

"I don't intend to get low marks, but I'll do something about it if I do." Bless him for his confidence. He had shocked me earlier as we chatted while walking among the boats at Fisherman's Wharf, telling me that he thought he could accept death by crucifixion if his crime was his beliefs. He'd had his first philosophy class and had met a monk that very day.

I pulled up to his building, and he hopped out. "I have to get my kettle from the trunk," he said. He had recently started drinking tea.

"Oh, I have a few other things for you," I told him. "Laundry detergent, computer paper, an extra pillow, and mugs." And all my love, I wanted to say.

I stepped out to hug him, but a few yards away, three female students had set up a booth to raise money for Hurricane Katrina victims. One of them had her head down reading, while the other two stared blank-faced over the green grounds. Without saying anything to me, Hudson walked over to engage them. He is philosophical but witty, too, and soon the three of them were laughing, which helped me hold back my brimming emotion. He returned to the side of the car. "Zoë always comes home for Thanksgiving, right?"

Hudson talks like that — an indirect question leading to the answer he needs. "Of course she does. I'll get you a ticket, too."

"And that's just in a month or so. So I'll see you then, Mom." My mistake. His reassuring tone was what he thought I needed. I whispered my goodbyes against his cheek, surprised again by the bristle of blonde whiskers.

"I'll miss you," I said. "I know you don't like to chat on the phone but send me some emails, hey?"

"Sure." He walked away, my seventeen-year-old son, a soon-to-be-discontented philosopher.

Chapter 9

Frozen Toothpaste Spit

"Mom, how do I know I'm not dreaming?"
"Because you are awake in the kitchen with me."
"How do you know you're not dreaming too?"

– Hudson, age five

When the kids were little, mornings for our family of six were stressful and chaotic. So why did I pine for them after the three oldest left home? It must have been the energy that I missed. Lily, Will, and I settled into our new routines. Will would wait for our teenage daughter to shower first — unless I'd seemed too edgy the previous day in my attempt to get her skinny butt out of bed, in which case he'd leave early to skip the threats and tension. Either way, Lily ate her cereal in the car while I drove her to school, and after her Cheerios, she brushed her teeth and spat her toothpaste out the car window, ready to do algebra with a minty fresh smile.

It was less organized when the kids were little and dependent on me to run the show, though there was a predictable rhythm to our chaos. Will and I would lie in our warm bed, still hanging on to dreams but aware of the red digital alarm clock ticking off the minutes. When it blared, he would shove it under the bed so that we couldn't see the flashing red numbers. If it was really late and every second was crucial, he would nestle it in the duvet beside us. "We've got to get up. We've got to get up," he always grumbled — motionless.

"I know, I know, I know," I'd say and, on cue, there would be our little Hudson at the bedroom door.

"Is it a school day?" he would ask, wiping away the water rolling down his forehead from his saturated cow lick. He would already be dressed in jeans and a sweatshirt and would have located socks in either the dirty laundry or the dryer. Back then, Hudson was our morning child.

I would assure him that it was a school day, swinging on my bathrobe and plodding downstairs without relieving my bladder or even splashing water on my face. Seconds were vital. Cole would have hauled his quilt off the top bunk and hunkered down in front of the TV to watch Rugrats. I would go into automatic pilot — new day, same words. "Cole, turn that off now. You know there's no TV until you're ready for school."

"But then there's no time." He'd roll off the couch and stagger into his room.

"Well, we all have to start getting up earlier," I'd say, the next lines in that well-rehearsed script.

"Yell at Zoë," I directed him automatically, but then tromped downstairs myself to sit on the edge of her bed. "Come on, sweetie," I'd urge, lifting the covers and rocking her shoulder. Amazingly, just as I'd be about to give her another nudge, the veil of sleep would lift, and she would get ready to join the din that was fast enveloping the house. I'd speed things up by tossing her clothes, but she would be considering her day and whether the outfit I chose would suit it. "Fine, do it yourself."

Cole, created in his father's image, would be calling for me to find him socks, while his dad, who denies he's ever made such a request, would be banging the dryer door and stomping about trying to locate the laundry basket. My bladder would demand that I pay attention to it, but not yet. Everything had to be in motion before I could afford to pause. Upstairs, Hudson would already have a bowl of Cheerios. If the milk carton was too full for him to handle, he would wipe up any spilled milk with a bath towel from the laundry room.

My legs would circle like the Roadrunner's as I located socks for Will who was anxious to make his exit and standing barefoot by the door in his suit and tie. (He's not a breakfast eater or brown bagger. Thank God.) I'd lay Cole's socks on the table (why were the mornings all about socks?) and grab a cereal bowl just as Cole asked for a grapefruit. It never seemed like adequate fuel on a chilly morning, but neither did cold cereal, and we clearly did not have time for anything hot. My morning routine would move into full swing. Slice the grapefruit, spin, and deliver. Search the refrigerator for the ham and mustard. Long stretch to the top of the stairs. "Zoë, are you coming up? You should be up here." Make a ham sandwich for Cole. Count: one lunch down, two breakfasts, no kindergarten snack. Zoë would come up, and I'd shove the Rice Krispies box her way. With everyone in motion, I'd race upstairs to use the bathroom, consider my disheveled state in the mirror for a split second, and run back down to the short order station to slap together a peanut butter and jam sandwich for Zoë's lunch. Ready before all of us, Hudson would suddenly be missing a school library book that, he'd urgently tell me, the teacher said he would have to pay for.

"What's on the cover?" I'd ask, and he'd try to remember, looking uncomfortably warm in his jacket, toque, and mittens, waiting for the others at the door.

"A green pig, maybe."

"It's under Lily's bed," Zoë would tell us.

"Don't wake Lily," I'd warn Hudson, but, of course, he would, and then she would be down making some unreasonable demand on me, like something to eat for breakfast.

Hudson would request an apple for his kindergarten snack, instead of the orange I was about to pop into the pack he was already wearing on his back. I'd take the stairs to the basement two at a time and find that the apples were wrinkled but would decide, if I approached from the back, I could get one into Hudson's pack unseen and then quickly throw in some cookies to compensate.

Cole had a little buddy who would call most mornings and offer a ride with his generous mom. I don't know if she was on to me, but I'd attempt to hustle all of mine out together so they could stuff themselves into her compact car. But then Cole would have lost a glove and Zoë wouldn't be able to locate her vinyl lunch bag, and, on cue, I'd say in an exasperated voice, "I've had it. This is crazy. From now on, you find all these things at night." Cole loved one particular pair of gloves so he would wear the one he had and put his other hand in his pocket, rather than search out a new pair. I'd grab a paper bag for Zoë's lunch.

"I hate taking paper. It's so wasteful," she'd protest.

"Bring it back, and I promise to use it over and over and over again."

By then, Lily would have joined our merry clan, asking for toast and jelly. "Not now," I'd tell her too abruptly, and she'd start to wail.

Zoë would spot her ecological lunch sack under the downstairs couch, and I'd toss in the goods and scoop up her coat. The neighbour's car horn would beep a friendly sort of "You hoo. We're here" reminder. Zoë was usually last out and always just about to pull on her hat when I would notice that her hair looked like small animals had burrowed in it, and race for the kitchen comb (once there was even kitchen toothpaste and toothbrushes in my endless attempts to do this better). Keeping the door open with one foot and hoping I wasn't exposing myself with my sloppy bathrobe, I'd tug the comb through her hair, one eye on the fully clothed and carefully groomed neighbour behind the wheel of the car she had probably heated up while she loaded the dishes from her boys' omelets into the dishwasher.

If the perfect neighbour wasn't picking them up, they would all make it out to the steps and ask, "Can we walk?" — meaning do we have time? I would say in a strained voice, "No, we have to change our ways," and then urge them on with, "Now run, run, run." As they took off down the street, I would call out, in as calm a tone as I could muster, "Bye, have a good day," because I felt strongly that something should be calm about their send-off. Many mornings, I'd have to act like a shepherd, blocking off the stairways into the nether regions of the house, shooing them along and prodding them out the door.

A proper cool-down routine was important. I knew I should keep moving and slowly clear up the debris of the hurricane that had just hit the house, but more often than not, I'd see that poor Lily had again been forced into self-reliance and made herself toast dripping with blueberry jam. So I'd collapse on the couch, bundling her onto my lap for a bit of the one-on-one time we both craved while I allowed her to feed me soggy toast.

It's weird but I did miss all that when I arrived home to a quiet house after driving Lily to high school. Sure, we still had our routines: Lily cranking up the radio with Green Day or the Black Eyed Peas while I lectured her on being late and pointed out that her toothpaste spit would still be frozen on the corner of Elbow Drive when she walked home from school. But it was different. Calmer. Still, Lily was fourteen and a half the autumn that Hudson started university, so I lived under the illusion that she would stay home for a few more years to feed my appetite for mothering.

Chapter 10

Sketchy Times

When you see someone putting on his Big Boots, you can be pretty sure that an Adventure is going to happen.

– A.A. Milne, Winnie-the-Pooh

There are photos and there are memories. Sometimes I confuse the two, but I recall so vividly the thrill and nervousness I felt in the airport as I hugged and kissed my mom and dad goodbye before departing on my first overseas trip. They looked at me like they couldn't stare at my face hard enough. I was eighteen and leaving on a three month backpacking trip around Europe with my girlfriend. Her parents and mine had us promise over and over again to call when we arrived in London, England. I made a brief echoing phone call upon my arrival in Britain to indicate that I had not disappeared over the Atlantic Ocean. Those were the last words we spoke to each other for three long months. We were close, my parents and I, but in 1977, no one talked long distance more than was absolutely required, and we couldn't pop into internet cafes and provide running commentary on our chaotic adventures. We sent postcards of the Loch Ness Monster and the lions in Trafalgar Square, as well as ones from obscure villages with names like Chambre d'Amour and Tomata that we slipped in and out of in France and Italy. Maybe those were the golden days of parent/child relationships, and we've fallen into a cacophony of communication. Now we pay our children's cellphone bills so they have to talk to us (and the two hundred friends they're connected with on Facebook).

At the age of seventeen and nineteen, neither of my boys was overly communicative. We talked when they were in the mood and didn't have more pressing matters, i.e. Sorry, Mom, I'm just (pick one) hanging out with a friend/trying to get some sleep/going to go for a run/late for whatever. It might have felt like rejection, sure, but I liked to think that they were within the normal range of boys that age when it came to co-operating with their mother's need for information and dialogue. So when did Hudson and Cole deem me worthy of lengthy communications with them? Simple, it was always when they needed help. When Cole set off on a trekking trip with a friend from grade school, not through Europe but the US of A, I might have lost less sleep and avoided some gray hairs if we could have returned to those pre-cell days of my youth in the seventies.

After a successful but uninspired term at university, Cole had decided to take a break. We'd given him a construction contract to help build our new family cottage in British Columbia, hoping that manual labor would encourage further schooling. Instead, with a bundle of hard-earned cash in the bank, he resolved that manual labor would not be his preferred way to make it in the world and began plotting his trip. The afternoon he left, Lily and I were sitting on the front deck in the warm autumn sun, commiserating on how great it seemed to be Cole just then. He had just finished packing up his friend's Chevy van. He had originally put everything in a suitcase, but his friend, George, had advised him to empty its contents into boxes in his well-organized van and leave the suitcase behind.

"Cole, do you guys have flashlights and extra water and candles — you know, survival equipment?" Only weeks before, Hurricane Katrina had devastated thousands of lives in New Orleans, and before he left for work, Will had lectured Cole on survival skills in the face of a natural disaster.

"Dad got us all that, Mom. Don't worry, we'll stay clear of Louisiana." The two boys shared a sarcastic grin and patiently posed leaning against the van, baseball caps tipped, while Lily took photos of their departure. They shooed her away and took off down the street, heading south toward the United States — the land they thought they knew from a thousand movies and episodes of South Park. The night before, they had abandoned their original plan to go to the US via Whistler and the west coast where they would have visited Hudson at his university residence in Victoria before taking a ferry to Seattle. That route was deemed too expensive. They would take the number two highway south instead, entering the US at the Sweetgrass-Coutts crossing, and wind their way east and south toward Salt Lake City, Utah, where Cole wanted to purchase a really tight video camera. Capturing events, or inventing them on video, had become a passion of his.

We received the first cellphone call a few days later — the lull before the storm. Will and I were driving to our partly finished cottage when Cole called to say they were in Salt Lake City. They planned to stay for a few days as Cole's bank only allowed him to get out eight hundred dollars a day and he needed nineteen hundred dollars to purchase the video camera of his dreams. He had the first eight hundred in his pocket but would have to stay two more days to accumulate the total amount, he told us. Was there any way we could help him get this money faster? It was late Friday afternoon, and we were on the road, too. We couldn't. Before hanging up, he enthusiastically told us that Salt Lake City was sweet, and the mountains there were epic — there were eleven different slopes to board on. "And listen to this," he said. "I went into this sick skate shop and was saying to the dude working there — man, it's weird, hey, everyone is

Mormon in this city. And can you believe it," Cole asked us, "the cool dude running the shop was Mormon, too?"

Two days later, Will was headed out the door on his way to work when a torrential downpour splashed rain back into the house. "Is there an umbrella in the closet?" he called back to me, and I handed him one from the high shelf.

"It might not work," I warned, and before I could holler at him to stop, he'd pushed the bent wires open. "I can't believe you just did that," I said, always surprised by his lack of regard for superstitions.

"I can't believe you care or that we're keeping this lousy umbrella," he said, smirking before ducking out into the storm.

Cole called from San Francisco that afternoon. (We had no idea they were headed that way.) He was captivated by the zealous energy of the city. They'd found a place to park the van cheaply until midnight each day, and after that, it was free. There were cool people everywhere. "But, man," he said, "everyone is gay here, hey?" And then he added, quoting Seinfield, "Not that there is anything wrong with that." (True — there are Mormons in Salt Lake City and gay people in San Francisco.) He'd bought a wicked video camera in San Fran that day, along with a tight insurance policy for it. I was suspicious of the insurance policy but said nothing. I held back from asking how much cash he had been carrying around as they travelled.

As trick-or-treaters disguised as Batman, Madonna, and Harry Potter bounced up and down our front steps the following night, we called Cole again, curious about Halloween in San Francisco. The two boys were at a huge gay Halloween parade along with thousands of costumed people, and he was getting sick video footage on his new camera, though they did slip down the wrong road at one point and things looked sketchy. I warned him to be careful about whose face he stuck that camera in. And please don't do anything sketchy. I didn't want to hear about sketchy.

Then Hudson, even less inclined to call to just chat, phoned from Victoria, making small talk while I waited for him to get to what was on his mind. He wanted to know if we would be okay with him dropping his two full term classes. He didn't like them, he didn't have the background he needed for them, and he couldn't possibly get a good mark in them. He would stay in the half term courses, he said timidly, only too aware of the tension his words were creating, and he would get a job to contribute to his education with the free time he would have. Of course, we weren't okay with it and told him that in no uncertain terms. It was then that he told us that his friend Marko from Calgary had moved out there, and the two of them were going to move into Will's sister and brother-in-law's basement. His aunt and uncle had offered that option to Hudson (not Hudson and Marko), because Hudson had irritably expressed how much he disliked living in residence. I reminded him that he had always had the option of living with his relatives but that his friend, Marko, did not.

On November first, I received another call from Cole. He told me that unfortunately things had got sketchy. George was not happy and said he needed to get out of San Francisco. He didn't feel well, couldn't sleep, and just wanted to return home. The boys, friends since forever, were arguing. Cole didn't want to end the trek, and so George had agreed to drop him at whatever mountain resort he wanted to go to. Cole told us, as if it was a feasible plan, that a guy he met back in Salt Lake City told him he could crash there.

I was beginning to dread phone calls. On the second of November, Cole called to tell me that — surprise, surprise — he couldn't, in fact, crash at the home of the guy he met in Salt Lake, so he had George drive him to Mammoth Mountain, California. The boys were getting along again, but Cole was intent on staying and George was heading home.

Now both my sons were calling. Hudson asked me to send him his resume from our home computer as he was applying for a job, just as he said he would. "Is a job really going to be better than another couple of university courses to replace what you dropped?" I wanted to know. "Why don't you replace the courses you didn't like with something you're passionate about learning?" I suspect my kids hate it when I start talking about passion — Hudson, especially. When pushed, Hudson admitted he didn't know if he wanted to stay in university at all once the term was up. Will had a business trip to Victoria planned and promised to take Hudson and Marko for a nice sushi dinner. My fingers were crossed that he would solve more of the mystery of what Hudson was feeling about school.

In the meantime, I sat on my hands to hold back from making too many calls to the wandering Cole. When I gave in, he told me that George was gone, and so he had slept in a really sweet hostel with a super comfortable bed. He was looking for work on the mountain, but he required a work visa. I suggested he continue to travel around — he could afford to do that — but he reminded me that he had a lot of equipment with him (snowboard, boots, helmet, and big camera) and, remember, no suitcase. Anyway, he loved it on Mammoth; it reminded him of Whistler. He'd met some guys from New Zealand and had gone skateboarding with a bunch of Americans. And he had met a woman on the street who said maybe he could live with her. (What?)

Will returned from Victoria and, even before plunking his suitcase down, told me Hudson and Marko wanted to get a two-bedroom apartment. He'd made them aware that they would have to sign a lease and would need first and last month's rent (they didn't know that). Will knew Hudson had planned this retreat from living in residence but suspected that even Hudson didn't know how long Marko would stick around Victoria.

By November fourth, Cole was referring to the people he'd met as his buddies. He said he'd met a nice Navajo guy who told him he got peyote for free simply because he was Navajo. (These phone calls were making me feel like I was also on an out-of-body trip.) The woman he'd met the day before, who he described as old, said he could live with her (he thought she was lonely). I cautioned my sociable son that this scenario seemed odd and to be suspicious. He quoted me something about riding two horses at one time — "you can't ride Faith and Worry both; you have to ride Aware." (Fine, I will ride Worry for him.) He also happily reported that he had met another dude who might drive him to Arizona to see the Grand Canyon. Not only that, but he had been offered a job bussing at a hotel restaurant, another job at a gym, as well as one at a skate shop — though all of them required a work visa.

Somehow, I allowed more than twenty-four hours to go by before I called Cole again. He told me that he had moved in with this older grandmother woman, and her adult daughter had visited the previous evening. "Of course, she came to check out who her mom let into her house," I cynically told him. Cole let on that he was sharing the woman's bathroom with her, which was awkward, and that the house was a bit of a mess but they (she and he) were cleaning it up — it was his idea. "How messy?" I asked. "Eccentric, scary messy?"

Even stranger than Cole being the one to organize a cleaning bee, his new landlady had never discussed rent. "And she isn't a cougar? Or a pedophile?" I asked.

"No." He was clearly exasperated with me. "You need to chill out, Mom. She's just friendly."

The next day, jolted by early morning worries, I called Cole and asked for an address, ranting about how nobody really knew where he was or what this suspicious woman was named.

"Come on, Mom. You have to chill out," he insisted again, but told me that her name was Debbie and she lived near Harry's Donut Shop in Mammoth Lakes where she drove a delivery truck. His living situation was the least of Cole's worries. "Hey, I'm trying to decide what to do here," he said. His savings would disappear swiftly if he paid the day rate to snowboard. He had the tricky dilemma of deciding whether to buy an entire season's pass for the hefty sum of thirteen hundred dollars, which would require him to stay and risk trying to get work that would pay him in cash, or choose an alternative plan like going back to Whistler, where he had heard there was already snow.

Leaving Cole to wrestle with that, I caught up with Hudson on his cell. He was walking alone on the beach and sounding miserable. "I guess I should have picked up more courses," he said. "Now I've got too much time on my hands. I'm going to get a part-time job."

"Find a job then, but keep up with your school work."

Silence. I tried again.

"I bet it's a gray day there."

"It's raining a bit, but I don't mind rain." He paused before saying the words I dreaded, "I just don't like it here. I don't feel like I should be in school right now."

"It's not the rain; it's the gray heavy sky that is getting to you," I equivocated. He was attending my alma mater where the charcoal clouds could hang over the campus, pressing on your psyche.

"Mu-um." I hated it when they said Mom with that two-syllable impatience, but finally I listened to the good parent fairy in my head that told me he needed me to empathize and confirm his feelings.

"Look, Hud, I do think things will get better. The first term isn't that easy."

"It's not hard," he said. "That's not it. I hate living in residence. I'm not in the right classes. It just seems like the wrong place for me now."

Breath deep, I instructed myself, trying to suppress my anxiety and the urge to vent. "Look, nothing is written in stone. Finish this term, Hudson. Do your best. If you decide you need to come home after this term, we can deal with that in December." The possible reprieve from everything that was weighing on him appeared to bring relief.

Having given Cole the opportunity to divulge what he was going through at seventeen when he left home to become a liftie in Whistler, and only learning from his essay that he felt like a young kid among older guys, I recently asked Hudson if he wanted to shed some light on his first months away from home. A few days after that invitation, he emailed me this revealing exposé.

I can't really recall why I decided to go straight to university rather than take a year off. I'm pretty sure it was mostly my aversion to working any sort of day job. It certainly was not a desire for higher education. I had become pretty disillusioned with all formal education during my last year of high school. I was always mistrusting of authority. I had a father who made sure his kids knew who the true enemy was — the government and, by extension, the government cronies: the police. School was something that came pretty easy to me. I was always what teachers would call a "smart kid." It never seemed to be something I should be particularly proud of. I didn't try that hard to excel at class. I just happened to be born with a natural aptitude for reading and writing, which was what the majority of kindergarten to grade twelve focused on. I learned at a young age that things should just come easy to me; if they're difficult, then I quit and find something I am naturally good at. I am still trying to overcome this tendency.

I was a very moody teenager. I had a sense that I was somehow the only one who understood how messed up the world was. I had an amazing girlfriend the summer before I went to university. We had been dating since the beginning of grade twelve. I had a crush on her since I first met her in grade seven. It was the kind of unrepentant crush that only someone who has never had their heart broken can have. I was a lovesick kind of kid. I really believed that my life would be perfect if I started dating this girl. Which is why I still have a hard time understanding why, after pining for her for over six years, when we finally kissed in the summer before grade twelve and it was the first time a relationship between us would actually have been possible, I told her I just wanted to be friends. I had literally been wishing to date this girl for more than half a decade, wishing on falling stars and holding my breath while driving through tunnels. Even when blowing out birthday candles, I was wishing for her to be my girlfriend. Then, when it finally happens, I tell her, "Naw, baby, I'm cool, let's just keep it casual." I am nothing if not afraid of commitment.

I told her I just wanted to be friends in the hallway of our high school, and later that night, after working out at the gym with my best friend and realizing what a knob I was being, I went over to her place all sweaty and in gym clothes and asked if we could date, and she said yes. We continued to date for the next year and a half with me breaking up with her a total of three times, every time for absolutely no reason whatsoever. She never cheated on me; I didn't break up with her for someone else. I just thought things would be better if they were different. This propensity for always thinking the grass is greener on the other side could adequately be used to sum up my academic career.

I spent most of the summer vacillating between whether or not I was going to go to university. I didn't like the idea of doing more school, something I had just left, but I also didn't like the idea of working. I've always been terrified of doing something I've never done before. Even up to this day, the unknown scares me. I recently had to buy car insurance for the first time, and the prospect was deeply unsettling. I always think someone is going to make fun of me for being clueless. It took me two hours to buy groceries the first time, because I was convinced the cashier was going to judge me on my selection of foodstuffs. So both going to university and not going to university were fairly daunting options. If I went, I would be living on my own, having to take care of myself and hardly knowing anyone in a completely new city. If I didn't go, though, I would most likely end up travelling. This meant I would have to take care of myself on a different continent, travel through different countries, and make thousands of decisions on my own every day. I really hate making decisions. University seemed to be an almost default setting so I went with that.

My girlfriend and I had decided not to do long distance so I was already in a bad place just leaving for Victoria. Although, to be honest, I am not really sure how upset I was about the whole thing. Sometimes I think I might romanticize our relationship in my mind because she is the only normal girl I have ever dated. Regardless, I was in a dark place when I headed out to UVic. I had enrolled at university and, this being Canada, not North Korea, I had made that decision of my own accord. Still, I would be lying if I said I was not heavily persuaded in that direction by a certain female parent of mine. I still don't know how to send an application to a university despite having been accepted to four, because honestly I never sent an application myself. I was always in the next room deeply not caring about the whole process. Thus it was easy to fool myself into thinking that I had been coerced against my own free will into going to school. If there is one thing I hate even more than making decisions, it is accepting responsibility for said decisions.

The courses I was enrolled in were almost all philosophy. I had yet to learn that studying philosophy in university is, rather ironically, a pretty much surefire way to give yourself an existential crisis. So I was at least somewhat excited, though hesitant, to start school. I mean, a class called "Philosophy of Mind" has to be pretty interesting, right? Spoiler alert: It's not. Oh god, how it's not. (Here's a question we studied for two weeks in that class: If a person has never seen the colour red before in their life but understood everything there is to know about the colour red, would they actually know what the colour red looks like? The answer is, of course: Kill yourself, your life has no meaning.)

Anyway, from the second I arrived, I was constantly debating whether or not to drop out. The main thing keeping me there was my friend Camilia, who kept me sane. She was a friend from high school. We went back and forth having crushes on each other, but things never timed up. I wish I could go back and tell my moody teenage self to just chill out and that it really doesn't matter what you do, life just goes on, but then again that's probably advice I wish my future self would give to my present self now.

That was Hudson, remembering himself at seventeen as too clever for his own good. Or maybe just clever.

On November seventh, Cole called to say he was in a car driven by a new buddy named Mosses (with Cole, there is always a new buddy). Cole had agreed to pay for the gas to and from Whistler if Mosses would drive him there. Mosses had never been to Canada and was psyched to see Whistler. They were in a car that belonged to his Navajo friend's sister. He (the Navajo guy) lent it to them. They were close to Seattle.

Only an hour later, Cole called to say they had a problem: Mosses had lost his driver's licence. The cops had stopped them on a busy stretch of highway in Oregon. Explaining the ownership of the car to the officer had turned into an overly complicated task. Once free to go, Mosses had driven off with his driver's licence in his lap, and it must have slipped to the ground at their next stop, which was now hours behind them. Cole sounded unruffled, but then Cole has a way of always sounding unruffled. Having lost his ID, Mosses' new plan was to drop Cole off at the border crossing closest to Vancouver. Trying to work it all out, Cole asked for Zoë's number to see if one of her friends with a car could pick him up at the border (his gear and belongings were in large plastic bags).

Another hour ticked by before Cole called to say they had reached the border, but things weren't good. Mosses drove too far forward in his attempt to drop him off and had entered Canada accidentally. Cole, now sounding decidedly ruffled, said he had admitted to the border guards that he was unable to find the receipt for the video camera he'd bought in the States and then stumbled — just for a minute, he emphasized — over the price. That was when they started to question him thoroughly, and now both he and Mosses, as well as the car and their bags, were being searched. Is this what I signed up for nineteen years ago? To help my kid, looking like a bag person, get back into the country? "Be polite and honest," I said. "Didn't we tell you to be careful at the damn border?"

"They're talking to me some more, Mom. Gotta go, Mom. Gotta go."

An hour later, a frantic Cole called again. "Look, Mom, I think I need to talk to Dad." I knew he was summoning his dad in his capacity as a lawyer, always a reason for alarm. "This has gotten sketchy."

Please, no. No more sketchy.

They were trying to trip him up; the customs agents had asked why he wasn't with the person he drove into the States with (maybe George saw all of this coming). Why, they wanted to know, did he not know how long he had intended to be away? Cole's luck wasn't working this time. I tried to get his dad on his work line but didn't succeed. Cole called again to inform me that he had spoken with the father of his good buddy, Brian, from Whistler, and Brian's dad had offered to drive to the border from his home in Vancouver and pick him up. God, I was grateful for Brian's dad and thankful for Cole's people skills, or things could have gotten far sketchier.

I was just recovering from that conversation when Hudson called again to tell us he had secured a job at a pizza place, and he wouldn't be able to come home for reading break the following day as planned.

"Are you sure, Hudson, you couldn't start in a few days? Don't you think you could use a break at home?" I didn't say a break from being seventeen years old and on your own for the first time, and unhappy with your courses, and maybe not sure you want to live with Marko. In case he changed his mind, I decided not to cancel his plane ticket until the noon deadline the next day.

Poor Lily was becoming the target of my frustration with her older brothers. On the drive to school, while she ate her Cheerios and brushed her teeth in the car (aiming, I believe, for yesterday's spit spot out the window), I lectured her on how if she wanted to pursue post-secondary education, she shouldn't even consider it until she had been out of high school for at least a year. And, furthermore, if she started university and wanted our help, she would have no choice but to finish it or not bother going at all. As I let her out of the car, she wisely told me not to take my shit with the boys out on her. Then Hudson called to say his new employer agreed that he could start after reading break, and so, yeah, keep the flight, because he could use a couple of days at home.

Cole called from Vancouver, where he was staying at Zoë's. He'd been to the American Embassy to apply for a visa to work in Mammoth, California. (Do they give visas to almost twenty-year-olds with job offers in skate shops?) He told me, in his usual even manner, that if he left the country, he would be afraid of the process of getting back into Canada. Then he finally sighed heavily and let me know how disturbing it was to have those border guards pat him over and then subject him to a two-hour interrogation. Worse was how badly he felt for his new friend Mosses who, never having really been here, now didn't want to come to Canada ever again.

"Come on, wrap your head around the whole scenario, Cole, and tell me if you would have let you into the country?" I asked him.

"Yeah, but after Brian's dad appeared, the customs dudes did a three-sixty in their attitude, suddenly trying to help me out by lowering the duty costs on the camera."

"Well, there are some advantages to being fifty," I said.

We picked Hudson up from the airport at 2:35 p.m. and slipped into our conversation that he didn't have to decide what he would do in January just yet. Home in the kitchen, I wrapped my arms around him, just a fast but solid hug for one of my boys. Lily and her dad made a big batch of popcorn, and we collapsed on the couch to watch a family favourite — Apollo Thirteen. Lily sat closer to her brother than she would have before he left, leaning against him as Tom Hanks prepared the Odyssey to re-enter Earth's atmosphere. The buttery popcorn, the movie lines we knew by heart — it was all backdrop for the comfort of being in the same room, thinking our own thoughts in a safe place. While I cooked up a batch of sticky chicken wings for Lily and Hudson, Hudson sat at the table and shared his desire to go to India or Tibet after he made some money by perhaps tree planting somewhere in BC.

Where once I could have been accused of helicopter parenting or hovering too close to my kids, at some point during that past week, I felt I was no longer guilty of that with my sons. Most of my friends' children were still at home at age twenty, certainly at seventeen. In those last few days, with Cole holed up in Mammoth, California, with who knows who and Hudson walking the beach trying to decide his own fate, I'd gained some perspective on the amount I could possibly influence these two offspring. They might be on circular or foggy paths, but they were making their ways. Though they'd reached out for some sort of solace, they weren't specifically asking for guidance. Somehow they had survived their troubles, the physical distance between us serving as a chance to experience independence.

The next afternoon, Cole called to say he had learned that Whistler wasn't even open yet, despite rumors otherwise. He thought he would come home to do another term at the University of Calgary, hang on to his current savings, and plan a trip in the spring. Could I survive the drama of our boys going travelling again? What sort of distressing phone call might I get from a kid in Tibet?

Chapter 11

Show Me Your Feathers

I wonder if I've been changed in the night? Let me think. Was I the same when I got up this morning? I almost think I can remember feeling a little different. But if I'm not the same, the next question is, Who in the world am I? Ah, that's the great puzzle.

— Alice in Alice's Adventures in Wonderland

Do you know that feeling when you are looking out the window but not seeing anything — not the snow heaped up in the yard, the bird on the phone wire, or the branches starting to stir with a late winter storm — and you realize life has changed? It's an odd feeling when you're suddenly aware that something isn't the same as before, even if you're not sure when exactly *before* was.

It can't be uncommon for children to tell their mommies, late at night during a bedtime hug, that they'll never, ever leave home. When Lily said it, she was probably six, and she hated to be left alone in her bedroom to go to sleep. One of those nights, after reading Ferber-type books on helping your child to separate for eight hours at bedtime and trying desperately to avoid tears again, I told her that part of growing up was spending the nighttime all comfy in her nice bedroom with Dad and me just across the hall. She scrunched up onto her pillow, wrapped her arms around her knees, and told me that she had decided that even when she had a husband and her own babies, they would all live with us. She would share her bedroom with them so that no one had to be alone. "That would be fine by me," I said, surprised she could feel so lonely with five of us in the house. Thinking back, I believe I indulged her fantasy and gave her permission to plan the reorganization of her bedroom into her future family's apartment, helping her decide where the baby's crib might go, where she and her husband could hang their jackets, and which part of the little room could serve as their kitchen. She was six and I was thirty-six the evening we struck that deal. But more than a decade later, I was staring out of the window, watching a little sparrow lift off the wire and disappear behind the neighbour's garage, while I tried to remember what I had been doing the day Lily, at fifteen years old, came home from school and began excitedly chattering about going on a foreign immersion program the following term of grade eleven.

The flight of the eldest three had left the baby of our family assuming responsibility for the *mother load*, i.e. me. Unlike her older sister, Zoë, who is inclined to avoid conflict, Lily is known for outbursts of sentiment. These aren't all negative; when she's happy, she exudes joy. High school was a rollercoaster of emotions for most of us, but more so for Lily. Though she had her small gang of teenage confidants, she was also willing to share the intensity of her feelings with me. Although not yet sixteen, her perspective was usually fairly mature, but then she had the luxury of witnessing half a decade of adolescent anguish, first loves, soul-crushing rejections, minor criminal activity, and mood swings in our lively home. As a result, except for occasionally ignoring homework, she was a fairly co-operative girl. Her siblings knew that, and I imagined, in their absence, they handed her a hefty mission: *Take time out from hanging with your friends once in a while and allow Mom to mommy you.*

It might keep a check on her email stalking. (This was just before smart phones and the texting boom, when we still had to make it back to our computers to email.)

Lily would often call at the end of a wintery school day and ask me for a lift home. My deal always was that I would help them get to school — I had a car in a household perpetually struck with early morning tardiness — but they had to find their way home from classes on their own. I figured the ten-block hike would clear their muddled heads. When Lily would call for a ride at three p.m., I'd perform the obligatory hemming and hawing, especially if she'd caught me halfway across the city, and then I'd cave in. Or, after she'd caught the C-Train downtown with friends to hunt for the newest must-have alternative rock CD or to peruse gypsy-wear in the vintage clothing shops, she would phone and ask, "Are you hungry, Mommy? Did you want me to grab us a table at that Latin place on Fourth we like or maybe our coffee shop on Thirty-third with the nachos and good lattes? I'll tell you about my day — I talked to that guy in math again. Is it a plan?"

When three or four of our kids were still living at home, I would have been too busy with my own obligations — writing school council reports, taking care of family bookkeeping, trying to astound my writing group, and carting in loads of food to feed the hungry hoards — to indulge in a slow meal in a restaurant with any of them. Fearful of being the overtaxed mom of media reports, I had attempted to limit my kids to two out-of-school activities each, reasoning that I might still be obligated to show up at eight places at any given time. Somehow, relying on help from other parents and even grandparents at times, I packed my car with water bottles, protein bars, wet wipes, and blankets for camping on the edge of soccer fields. I raced between the kids' after-school activities: Zoë's piano lessons and musical theatre, Cole's baseball practices and guitar lessons, Hudson's soccer games and karate instruction, and Lily's basketball games and choir practices. Media articles told me I should have felt overtaxed and underappreciated. Maybe I did at the time, but now that it is over, I know I liked the fast pace and the energy involved. That said, there was upside to having only Lily at home.

I'd been known, on occasion, to direct the rest of the family to be cautious of how we treat the baby of our clan who, like a typical youngest child, may be *slightly* spoiled. "Don't indulge her. You're not doing her any favours," I'd say. But the tables had turned. One afternoon, Lily overheard me joking over a cup of tea with a neighbour whose kids had yet to fly the coop. "This is what I suspect happened," I said. "When Lily's siblings made their whirlwind visits home at Thanksgiving, they took their baby sister aside and, to keep my swarm of emails at bay, they whispered to her, 'Do us a service, Lily. Let Mom buy you lunch once in a while. Tell her your troubles. *Indulge her*. Really, it's good for her — and us.'" In response to my friend's laughter, Lily stuck her head into the kitchen and categorically told me that our mid-week dates were her idea, before stomping off to her bedroom with a bowl of Cheerios.

In fact, those dates on Fourth or Thirty-third with my dramatic youngest detailing her day while we sipped virgin margaritas or steaming lattes were occasions I wouldn't have forsaken for the world. The truth was this new arrangement, voluntary or not, worked for both of us — which amplified my shock when Lily first mentioned the foreign immersion program.

I feared that if her application to study abroad was accepted, by January, Will and I would be living in an empty house, and our lives would look dramatically different: no more hanging with parents on the sidelines of a basketball court, no more lattes on Fourth. I didn't come to this conclusion on my own. Our friends and family couldn't shut up about the impending possibility of an empty nest. What was with that? Were they all watching to see how we would replace the noise and chaos, comings and goings, organizing and meal planning, and endless discussion that goes on when you have kids at home? Were they waiting to see how we would manage when too many of our evenings and weekends became unfathomably quiet? Their curiosity was well founded. I pondered that uncertain future along with them.

I might have suggested we take up ballroom dancing if we hadn't already tried that. Around ten years into a marriage, it is apparently what wives get their husbands to do. It felt like a coup when Will agreed. Turns out his not wanting to do it didn't translate into him not being *able* to do it. Will foxtrotted, two-stepped, and cha-cha-chaed across the gym floor with ease, sometimes with the male instructor, after it became clear that I was unteachable. I sympathized with Hudson, who used to beg me to let him quit each activity he chose to do — music lessons, karate, *and* baseball. Taking a page from my book, Will made me stick out our lessons to the last ungainly swing dance.

One of Will's younger work colleagues suggested we get a puppy. Her parents had *fostered* puppies when she and her siblings all left home. She couldn't know that Will and I are considered by some of our nearest and dearest to be anti-pet. These friends have been known to get all misty-eyed and accusatory, and say things like *well, I know you don't like my dog.* Hey, if I lived out in the country, I might acquire a dog to protect me from those things that go bump in the night. But after raising four kids and changing a zillion diapers back in the day, I firmly decided against doing the doggie poo thing (and maybe the hair on the couch, slobber on my leg, and kibbles everywhere.) Okay, Will and I don't really *care for* (as one of Lily's friend's mom taught her to say, instead of *I hate)* all things doggy. So no ballroom dancing or puppies would fill the emptiness we might feel *sans kids* at home. Will had given up golf half a dozen years earlier. The year I turned forty-seven, I took lessons in both knitting and outdoor in-line skating. In-line skating was okay, but I've yet to find an in-line skating partner. Knitting and purling passes the time on planes and long drives, though Will confessed that while he's aware that young people knit, watching me knit made him feel old. That same year, Will bought his dream machine — a midnight blue sports car. He failed to understand that driving in the low-slung car made *me* feel old. I had to concentrate to gracefully get in and out, but also, I tried to explain to my oh-so-proud husband, I was all too aware of the double-take pedestrians gave us as we drove down the street, radar detector on, seventies music blasting. It said, *Hey, was that an old guy who can finally afford a cool sports car playing old guy Led Zeppelin tunes, and if it was, I don't have to be envious because I'm not old yet.* (Glance again.) *Yes, he was old for sure. Oh, and look, his wife is knitting.* Perhaps we could be diverted from our empty-nestedness by planning two-seater driving trips to places old people go — Victoria, Yellowstone Park, and Mount Rushmore — while I knitted tiny, lopsided sweaters for Zoë's friends' new babies.

As fate would have it, after his first term, eighteen-year-old Hudson continued to feel like he didn't know what the heck he was doing at university. He was still confused about what he wanted to study and couldn't get used to living in a dorm, among other justifications for how, at seventeen-and-a-half, he just hadn't been ready to go away to school. (No kidding. I agreed now.) He was returning from Victoria via a trip to the Kootenay region in southern BC. "I just need some time to think," he called to say late one evening, in a tone that was too quiet and even. He followed that with, "Don't worry about me," ensuring we would worry about him. A few days later, he called to say, "I'm considering going into an ashram. It's cheap. You just have to do laundry for them or help with meals or whatever, and you can meditate and, you know, think." This from the kid who wasn't much into doing his own laundry and avoided cooking as much as possible. (Hudson had shared that while he could imagine being a stay-at-home parent, his future wife would have to do all the cooking or he would live off peanut butter toast forever.) And this was our philosopher son, who, without the calm and peace of an ashram, found time to reflect, deliberate, and ruminate himself into a *thinking funk* often enough. We held our collective breath as Hudson went non-communicative in a youth hostel near the ashram, trying to decide if he wanted to enter. Perhaps he would find something he was missing there.

Still I worried about not hearing from him until he walked in the door one morning with his own laundry, after boarding a Greyhound bus home late the previous night, having decided not to sign up to do other people's washing.

Considering Hudson's torment, I figured that my approach to Lily's request to do the immersion program had to be completely hands off. I did not want the blame should she call from a faraway place to say she was so sad and lonely. Maybe the foreign immersion idea would fade away, as teenage ideas often do, and be replaced with another half-baked scheme. But Lily was a take-charge kind of girl and had the whole application process rolling neatly along on her own, right up to arranging for all of us to be interviewed at home as part of the in-depth study of the prospective applicant.

A serene young woman from the cultural immersion organization showed up at our house to handle the interview. She asked Lily to tell her what sort of rules we have in our household. Lily leaned forward, narrowing her brown eyes in concentration. Will and I held our breaths. And, sure enough, instead of choosing any of the random rules that govern our home (*inform me before you borrow my car, phone when you're out past one a.m., our family eats pizza on Friday night*), Lily went a different direction. Back during the wild heyday of Zoë's high school musical theatre involvement, our home had been the place to congregate on Friday and Saturday nights (occasionally Thursdays and Sundays, too). Close to the opening night of *Joseph and the Amazing Technicolor Dreamcoat*, I remember feeling that some of Zoë's school friends were taking advantage of the largesse of our hospitality. In other words, our place was turning into party central. (Had I gone wrong providing all those bowls of chips and pretzels and stocking up on salsa in an effort to make sure I knew where *my* kids were?) One morning, I woke up to hard evidence of underage drinking — beer and vodka bottles in the back alley trash can. Furthermore, one of Zoë's girlfriends, who had a notoriously strict mother, was sound asleep with *Joseph*, of the technicolor coat, in Zoë's bed.

Thankfully, both were fully clothed. That girl's mom would have slaughtered us if she thought we condoned such a thing. Rules for our house were immediately posted on the basement door for the duration of the musical. Lily chose to share one of those with the nice lady doing the interview. "Oh, I know a rule we have. Boys and girls who aren't related aren't allowed to sleep together here anymore."

After the crimson left our faces and we stuttered out some explanation for what the brat was talking about, the interviewer indicated that it was a wrap. The interview process was a safeguard against families who were really whacked out, she said, and ours was, of course, fine.

"Hang on," I wanted to shout, "this kid is too young, fussy, protected, small..." I wondered what I would have to say to stop the whole ridiculous plot.

Prego. They found Lily to be a well-rounded candidate and decided she could go to a little Italian village (little sounded safe). Lily begged them to let her go to a city, urban girl that she was, and they complied, congratulating her on being accepted to an Italian language and cultural immersion program in Rome. For five whole months, she was going to live in one of the loveliest areas of one of the loveliest cities in the world. Trastevere is one of the last pockets of medieval Rome, and Lily would live there in the home of a family with whom we had only exchanged a few brief emails. She would have a *host mother and father*. Will and I had been replaced.

As we drove that long, winding road to Calgary's airport, it was Lily's turn to listen to me share my memories of the day I flew to Europe when I was eighteen. I told her how thrilled I was setting out to hostel around a foreign continent with the girlfriend who helped me get through grade twelve math, my parents left behind, anxious and fretting. But more fresh in my mind, I told her, was the afternoon four years ago when I drove a nervous Zoë to the airport to leave home for art school orientation in Vancouver. I couldn't stop hanging onto Zoë, not wanting to let her go from the security of my arms to airport security. Just as clearly etched in my mind was the morning we drove Cole and his friend, Hugo, to the airport so that they could start their not-quite-adult lives in Whistler as lifties.

Hudson was back home now, but it had only been a few months earlier that I had taken *him* to the airport so that he could fly off before me to attend orientation for the University of Victoria. When Hudson had left, I had been stunned at how fast it was all happening. I would have cried again if I tried to tell Lily what a mess I had been as Hudson hefted his pack onto his broadening shoulders and told me, "You'll be okay, Mom," before turning toward security. (It shook me up even though I was driving his belongings and computer out to him after he finished his orientation.) Seeing those three off had left me sad and pensive on the long drive home and for days afterwards. I'd been overwhelmed by the significance of those moments, sensing they were the culmination of a journey.

Those goodbyes were momentous, but they weren't the end, or even the middle. Zoë, the first to leave, came home for the first two summers to live with us again. I loved to watch her wander in the back gate at the end of a sometimes stressful shift as a lifeguard. She would stop to poke through the garden to replete her energy with a handful of ripe raspberries. It wasn't until after her third year that she harangued us into reluctantly agreeing to let her spend her summer in Vancouver. She promised to work long hours to pay her rent and contribute to her university costs. She had broken up with her high school boyfriend and though I was sad to see him leave the place he had in our family, she had met another fine young man, an art student like herself, who aspired to become an architect. She was living the way she wanted in a house full of dramatic artists. Both Will and I argued adamantly that she should continue to spend her summers at home, living rent-free while earning funds to contribute to her university expenses. How could we just let her live away year-round? I remember kneeling in our back garden, a small spade in one hand, my cell in the other, digging up the first spring weeds while I listened to my closest girlfriend convince me that it might be alright to let Zoë, at age twenty, establish a life away from our home. My instinct was to protest, as I upturned tender new dandelions, but she convinced me to loosen my grip. God, what would I do without my smart girlfriends?

Cole had worked (and played hard) for two seasons in Whistler, intermixed with terms of university. Each time, he grew up more, managing his own simple meals, undertaking limited housekeeping, arranging transportation around town, and generally developing *getting-by* skills. Hudson was back home searching for his niche after that one mixed-up term at university. Now, Lily, the baby of the family, was flying the coop.

"Zoë was eighteen and the boys were seventeen when they left," Lily said as we pulled into an airport parking stall. "Can you believe I'm doing this and I'm only sixteen?"

"No," I told her, "I can't believe it. I should have said no at the beginning."

"Lots of parents would have said no," she replied, as she helped haul her two giant red suitcases out of the trunk, not realizing how seriously I was considering why the hell I went along with this proposal from its inception. Lily was organized, motivated, and, I hoped, fairly sensible. She was a kid who, simply put, got things done (not always things we approved of). Whole books have been written about her type of personality. She is what you call *a sensitive person*: sensitive to other people's moods, to the clothes she wears, to the food she eats, and especially to the lighting of a room. How could I have agreed to her spending five months in a strange home in a foreign culture; why would she even seek that out? I reassured myself by thinking of a theory I read years ago when I first began to worry about her adaptability. The theory was that these sensitive kids are, in fact, the ones who grow up to seek out adventure and new challenges, because, having been forced to adapt all their lives, they actually feel up for it. That theory was a bit hard to get my mind around at the time. If you don't know someone like Lily (and you probably do), you might think she is just fussy. I don't think that's the case. It seems to me that while so many people are willing to go along with things in life, people like Lily strive to seek out the best circumstances for themselves, and they acutely feel their disappointment when it doesn't work out.

Lily has learned that ordering chicken quesadillas in a restaurant almost always works out for her. Of course, she checks to make sure the onions are green, not white. She has told me that the biggest issue is the chicken — "it has to be the kind of chicken that rips in strips, not that weird white chicken that has been cut into neat little cubes. Anyone would agree that stuff is gross." (If the onions *are* white or the chicken *is* square, she switches to pepperoni pizza, though she prefers the pepperoni on top of the cheese, please.) This daughter, who went out of her way to seek out well-lit interiors, who spoke some French, but very little Italian, and who worried too much about who liked her, had decided to immerse herself in a faraway land on the other side of the Atlantic Ocean. There, she would be surrounded by strangers speaking a foreign tongue who may or may not *like* her and would likely abide in shadowy, ancient homes. Still, she had spent a season walking home from school, hugging the last rays of sun on short winter afternoons, listening to Italian CDs. She had experimented with different pastas, and she had agreed to try *inner crying*, rather than sobbing out loud when circumstances defeated her. She couldn't wait to see what everyday life in Rome had in store for her. Lily was an amateur photographer — what amazing settings the *Colosseo*, the *Fontana Di Trevi*, and the *Piazza Navona* would be for her art.

It's true she had cried in public places, but joy could overcome her, too. She'd been known to skip in public, burst into song, or make candid observations to random people. "Try not to be a weirdo," I said as we headed for the airport check-in counter.

"Don't worry, Mom," she replied, understanding perfectly what I meant. "I will be *so* on the level." She made a broad gesture with her hand, slicing straight and even through the air. "*So* on the level."

I had been tempted to warn her *host mother* that my daughter got overwhelmed easily. But I had held myself back. "They're Italians," my Italian friend said. "They understand emotion." Of course, I would also have told them how Lily could be sunny and helpful, and how thrilled she was when she captured the perfect photo on film.

Will was unable to come to the airport, but the previous evening, the three of us had gone out to dinner, and he had given Lily a crash course on personal safety, making me quiver in my snow boots. Normally, Lily would dismiss her father's concerns, impatiently telling him she knew it all before stealing off to her room to listen to a Moldy Peaches CD. But over our plates of pasta, Lily could perhaps smell her dad's animal fear, and she met his nervous stare with dark brown eyes. "You don't have to worry, Daddy. I'll be smart." Through strict safety instructions, her dad hoped to fend off any boogeymen in Italy; Lily and I would have preferred not to think of it while we tried to eat our linguini marinara in Calgary.

Hudson had come along for the ride to the airport, though he hadn't said much during the drive. Due to childhood jealousies and competitiveness, Lily and Hudson had spent too many of their early years not getting along. There had been days when I listened to them bicker on and on until I threatened to haul them off to family counselling. Yet, amidst the comings and goings of Zoë and Cole, Hudson and Lily had kept to their truce. Even if the peace was merely the result of needing an ally at home, it was a blessing.

As we neared the security clearance, I believe Hudson felt like his dad, protective and scared for the safety of his little sister. He looked sad preparing to see her off. "Hey, Hud, you can come visit me. Save as much as you can from your job. Live cheap. You can do it." Hudson shrugged and silently hugged her hard. I slipped a greeting card into her purse, far too emotional to express my feelings out loud. I held her thin shoulders tightly before handing my fourth child over to airport security.

Without even considering the boogeyman/stranger risks that haunted Will, I was fearful for how it would all go. Zoë and I had drawn up odds and thought there was a one hundred percent chance that Lily would phone in tears hating more than one aspect of her adventure. Zoë gave it a seventy percent chance, and I gave it fifty, that Lily would want to come home before five months were up, though we had insisted that we expected her to stick it out. Tears or not.

The morning that she left, I'd stood at the kitchen counter, my hands trembling, imagining Lily getting up and eating breakfast with her unknown Italian family, and so I had written, "I am so proud of you," in the card she would be opening high above the snowy fields of Alberta. And I was. So proud. In that fluttery, letting go way that tugged at my heart.

Chapter 12

The Unbearable Weight of Being Misunderstood

Mom. Calm down. You get more bees with honey. I'm not giving you any bees until I have forgotten how irritating that email was.

– Email from Lily in Rome

Sixteen-year-old Lily leaving home to live with a mysterious family in Italy turned out to be *una grande* parenting challenge. Lily had never minded checking in with me and sharing (most) of what was going on in her world. Because I didn't want this to change with her overseas, I was uncomfortably challenged to hold back from reacting too harshly when she divulged details that our other kids would never have dreamed of disclosing. Guiding her through her often impulsive, sovereign exploits was oh-so-taxing.

Almost all of Lily's contact with home during her Italian immersion program was through email. I was happy that she emailed almost daily, but, Lily being Lily, her missives were often laden with anxiety and had me practicing my best remote parenting. At just barely sixteen, in such an unfamiliar situation, Lily needed guidance from me and her dad. Of course, my headstrong daughter didn't agree. We found out quickly that parenting loses its punch when you're a continent away from your child. When you say, "Hang out with your host sister instead of that stranger you met on the bridge," and your honest daughter tells you that there is no way she is going to comply with that rule, it's almost impossible to enforce consequences.

So we bickered via email. I was forced to make great strides in the art of the *consoling* email, and we gave each other a sense of our lives on either side of the Atlantic Ocean. Lily informed me that she had found a place to go to cry out loud, and during those five months, she had plenty of reasons to go there. As I adapted to her absence, her emails kept her close.

Date: January 30
Subject: I've arrived Mommy

Wow, I'm here and it is amazing. The family picked me up at the train station yesterday and gave me a little bouquet of white roses! And can you believe their flat is above una Libreaire del'cinema — an independent book and DVD store — which is so cool I can't even begin to explain how cool it is.

Julia (my host) and I have been out walking. This neighbourhood, Trastevere, is beautiful. When Julia and I stepped out of the building, two men passed us, and one said to the other, "Che belle le ragazze, sì?" Mom, I am going to get molto di più tough to contend with these men.

My host mom speaks more English than I expected. But I have a feeling this family is a little more... I don't know. I think that they might impose rules on me that I'm not used to. I hope that doesn't sound too negative... Miss you, mummy

TI AMO lily

Date: February 1
Subject: Rules

Come on, Lily. I know you'll have no problems going along with their rules — remember Rome is a big city with so many more outsiders or wandering people in it than Calgary. (You can't trust those wandering souls.)

I loved hearing your impressions of Italy when you called — the shutters, the Vespas, the big ancient door keys.

My friends are taking me out for lunch and I think the reason is "since I must miss you." Which, of course, I do, but I will be just fine about it. You are on a great adventure.

Love, Mom

Date: February 1
Subject: Hey real family

This family dynamic reminds me of ours. There is a mom who knows what's up and does a lot. A dad who puts the "chicken" on the table and is very smart. The older boy wants to be a cinematographer and they say that he is "like a tornado," whirling around and mixing it up — so like Cole. I've only met the younger brother once, but he seems perceptive and self-contained the way Hudson is. I don't know if they have a Zoë or a Lily. (I like Julia but we're quite different... she loves the radio.)

Please send me a good recipe for pancakes (i only know how to make them from the box) so i can make my host family some, and they can use the Canadian maple syrup you insisted i bring.

Ciao Lily

Date: February 4
Subject: scared

Mom, I'm so scared of getting fat here! Every time i sit down, I never want to stop eating, because everything tastes so great. And all we eat is cheese and bread and meat, which can't be very good for me.

Lily

Date: February 4
Subject: Re: pancakes

Look around you — do you see many fat Italians? And remember you're doing all those stairs. I'll see if I can find you the best pancake recipe. Email me photos.

love you, Mom

Date: February 5
Subject: wanted to hide away

I can feel myself starting to cry just thinking of how to write this email. I'll try not to elaborate too much — this morning my host mom took me to my school to give them some documents, and I had to speak with some of my new teachers. By the time we got back to *this home*, I was feeling so homesick for my *real home*, because it's so scary having to pretty much start my life all over like this.

By this afternoon, i was wishing that i could just hide away until this starts being fun, but obviously it doesn't work like that. But i only had to wait a few hours for things to be better. We went to one of Julia's friend's places, then out for pizza. Met some others, Rosa (nice and pretty cool), Livia (laughs a lot which i like — really jokey), and Maria (sort of puts her guard up). No one really talked to me except for Julia's brother — he wanted to talk about Canada though, so it was boring. But it was good to go out and see what Roman teenagers do on a Saturday night (not much yet).

Oh, and i made the pancakes this morning. They turned out sweet. Tell the aunties that i said thanks for the recipes.

Love, Lily

Date: February 6
Subject: Be brave

Hi Sweetie,

Hey, you. You have to be brave and talk to Julie and her friends. That's what you are there for. Use sign language if you don't have the vocabulary yet. You should email your big sister. She's feeling the stress of her looming grad project. Talk to her about how much she'll enjoy seeing Rome and Italy — and you — when we visit there in the spring and graduation is behind her.

Ciao and kisses, Mom

Date: February 7
Subject: The unbearable weight of being misunderstood

Okay, so julia and i take the 63 bus to school. This week was a terrible one to start classes, because it's some kind of student takeover. When i arrived yesterday, there were no students there! My English teacher was rude to me and told me to come back at 9:00. I was going outside, and the "doorman" stopped me. He didn't speak English, so how could i explain myself? A teacher brought me to the administration hall, and all these teachers were staring at me while a woman spoke in French to me because i said i speak *some* French, and she was *insisting* that another teacher was going to take me back to my class.

Mom, I was like, "Yeah! I know that's what he's trying to do, but I was there *already*, and the teacher there told me to leave!" Still he brings me back upstairs where my English teacher again treats me like an idiot and is like, "Don't you understand? I told you to come back at 9:00." I told him that i understood perfectly.

It was really awful, mom. All these people were treating me like an idiot when *they* were the ones who couldn't understand what was happening. So after I ended a long and humiliating conversation with my English teacher, I went across the street and bought some tea. I asked for fruit tea, but they didn't understand so they just gave me English Morning tea — because I'm one of those pesky English people. I hardly drank any of that and then went back to school. Three other classmates were there so we spent the next two classes talking with our biology and philosophy teachers. Well actually they were all talking in Italian so I was just standing there.

Mom, the whole morning all I could think was that I really should've gone to France. It would've been way easier. There was a break, and I ended up joining a fifth year class. The boys in that class were loud and immature. It's ridiculous that they keep doing school for 13 years. There are 19-year-old boys in high school! And notice i said *boys*, not men, which is what they should be by that age.

Though there was one boy that seemed pretty sane. We talked a bit because he was reading *The Unbearable Lightness of Being*. And he *was* cute.

Lily

ps. I can't wait to show Zoë everything I'm here to discover.

Date: February 7
Subject: Oh Baby, you crack me up.

You should have phoned from the principal's office so I could give them a piece of my English-breakfast-tea mind. Honey, it can only get better.

We are over the moon about seeing you in May, just have to coach Zoë into not coming undone over her grad project so that can be behind her when we travel.

Dad and I are escaping bitter winter weather to a conference he has in Las Vegas. I am SO looking forward to sitting around a pool drinking pink drinks with umbrellas in them. (Not being stressed out by kids contemplating an ashram, undertaking an overzealous grad project plan, or being bullied by non-tea-drinking Italians.) Gotta go put fake tanner on my lily white legs for Vegas.

Ti Amo, Mom

Date: February 12
Subject: the unbearable weight of waiting to hear from Lily

Lily, I know it is Sat. there and I hope you're out and about having fun, but I am worried because I haven't heard from you since you mentioned the tension between you and Julia when you emailed Dad's Blackberry in Vegas. I would love to hear that you have a handle on that and have realized this is the relationship that you both need to go smoothly. Really, Lily, it is. I know I said I'd shut up, but then I haven't heard and, of course, shutting up is hard for me.

Talk to me, Lily.

Mom

Date: February 12
Subject: don't freak out

Things are fine. There's a good system working itself out. No worries. I met this boy, Mika, from Prague tonight. Don't freak out. He is just this really sweet, intelligent boy who is staying in a hostel in Rome. He's kind of a wuss. The guys I was going to go to the soccer game with couldn't get me a ticket, which was a good thing because they ended up getting in a car crash. (They're okay.) So I spent my Saturday night hanging out with Mika eating pizza and ice cream at the Spanish Steps and the Pantheon, and today (Sunday) we walked along Lungotevere to the Vatican.

So I am finding things to do on my own and Julia goes out on her own, and we're getting along swimmingly now. No more social clashes.

Mom — about calling you, I'm sorry but I need to save my last few minutes on my phone card to call Daniel in Calgary on his birthday Tuesday.

Ciao, Lily

Date: February 13
Subject: 16 years/three weeks

Go get another card, because I think we need to talk. I will pay. In fact, if you don't call me, I won't put your last paycheck from Food Market in the bank, or your tax rebate (400 smackers), or another red cent. How do you like those apples?

The way I see it is this. Daniel has been your *sort of* boyfriend since just before you left — so three weeks. I have been your mom for 16 years. Can't wait to chat.

Good to hear that you are getting along swimmingly with Julia, but it didn't sound like Julia was going to the soccer game (thank God they couldn't get you a ticket) or, of course, out with the Mika guy from the hostel. Lily, it is just what Dad and I asked you NOT to do — go off with people you don't know from Adam. I'm glad he was nice and intelligent, and I might even be glad that he was a wuss. I know you have an independent streak in you — which is good — but given your circumstances with Julia, independence can be rude, too.

Waiting for that call, mom

Date: February 13
Subject: My heart sank when I read them

Mom. Calm down. You get more bees with honey. I'm not giving you any bees until I have forgotten how irritating that email was.

Lily

Date: February 13
Subject: harder than I thought

Lily, email can cause problems because so much of what is really going on can't be shown. Like how much I miss you today, even if I am being bossy. I don't want to "make your heart sink." It is harder for me than I thought having you so far away.

Love, Mom

Date: February 13
Subject: Mom — Chill Out

Mom, I need you to get used to not knowing my every coming and going. I'm going to call Daniel for his birthday first, because I don't want to run out of minutes in the middle of our conversation. I'll get a new card and call you after that. You only have to wait two more days of not hearing my voice.

I appreciate your advice, but I would be much happier to receive emails from you that offer me little tidbits of love, not criticism. I know your criticism is backed by love, but I'm talking about straight-up love — like telling me what you're making for dinner at home or telling me my room still smells like me and my CDs are still there.

Tell me when it snows. Lily

Date: February 14
Subject: orange peels and you

Lily, sorry but no one asked me to sign off mothering my sixteen-year-old while she's gone (note: I said mothering, not smothering).

The Chans are coming for dinner, and I'm making salmon linguine, warm walnut salad, a chocolate pecan tart, and bruschetta the way they make it in Italy — rubbed with garlic. Your room definitely still smells like your orange peel collection and you. And your CDs are there.

Kisses, Mom. Hey — what about that photo? Why won't you email a photo?

Date: February 14
Subject: News for the Fam — for Mom to share

Hey everybody. Here's what's up:

I'm living in one of Rome's most happening neighbourhoods, Trastevere. Ristorantes, cafes, bars, clothing stores, gelato shops, the works. I live close to a beautiful square called Piazza di Santa Maria. If you go there at the right time in the afternoon, it fills with sunlight, and there's a huge fountain in the middle where people sit, read, talk, smoke, meet up, eat ice cream, and make out. It's real cute. I love going there just to people watch and soak up the sun.

The best place for watching the sunset is a hill called Gianicolo. I love walking there (some very epic things on the way). If you sit on one side of Gianicolo, you can watch the sun fall behind these tall green trees off in the distance and glimpse the gardens of some extremely expensive houses and St. Peter's church lit up in pink. On the other side, I watch the rest of Rome start to light up for the night and the sky grows darker and darker blue.

I love getting and giving kisses on the cheeks all day!

Hold down the fort for me. Love, Lily

Date: February 21
Subject: Mommy? Mommy?...

Are you doing some sort of thing where you don't respond to my emails to show me how much I need them? Like those times when you didn't clean the house to see how messy we would let it get? Some kids at school are telling me that the Canadian women's hockey team won a gold medal in Turin, Italy, the other day. Cool, if you are into that sort of thing.

Zoë finally emailed me. She sounds neurotically introspective as usual.

Love, Lily

Date: February 21
Subject: Sisters, sisters (sung)

I would never stop emailing you to make a point. I need to email you to not miss you so much. It was Family Day Monday so we took Cole and Hudson snowboarding — you wouldn't have liked it; it was ridiculously cold. Dad says to remind you to take your host family out for lunch. Yeah, the Canadian women beat Sweden 4 to 1, after Sweden beat the US women. Are you watching the Olympics in Italian? And come on, Lily, please send me photos of you in Rome.

Love lots, Mom

Date: February 27
Subject: this email is stressful even to write. Be a nice Mommy and write back in a calming way.

Yes, I will take my host family out for lunch, but it's honestly going to be hard. There are very few times when everyone is available, and I'm sort of feeling like every time I open my mouth, my hosts feel like I am a burden. If I suggested that we all go out to lunch on Sunday or something, my treat, it would be really hard to get the "my treat" part across. My host mom almost always speaks to me in Italian now so communicating is getting harder.

I've been contacted by the other girls who are in Rome on exchange. They want me to meet them for lunch Tuesday (they all know each other because they took Italian lessons together and have been here for four months). They are going to try to give me tips and force me to give my reactions about being here, and it's just going to be the same old getting-to-know-a-stranger exercise that i am starting to hate.

This weekend, I went to see a photo show at the American Academy of Rome and then to hear a new beatmaster with my neighbour, Juno. The music and dancing were sweet, but it was awkward because I think Juno has a crush on me.

Lily

Date: February 27
Subject: Shshh there, there now

Shshh there, honey — Mommy's here. Everything is going to work out. (How's that for calming?) Now down to business — you know without me saying that you should go to lunch with those girls. To spend five months in a country where you don't know anyone, you have to get used to getting to know strangers (oops — I don't mean I want you to hang out with total strangers from hostels).

If you honestly think it would be hard to take your hosts out, then you could bring treats back to the flat. Buy some nice fresh fruit and croissants, and pick up some flowers.

Relax and try to be yourself, and everyone will treat you well — your host family, the exchange girls, and, yes, Juno, too.

Love you more than Juno could, Mom

Date: February 28
Subject: good mom to the rescue email.

Wow, good job, Mom. On Sunday, I'm making French toast for everyone. I picked up the bread today and helped with dinner last night — everything's copasetic. Keeping my chin up. Might even take the photos — but I'm afraid they just won't capture what I want. Can you believe some dude downloaded the billionth song from iTunes and won a $10,000 iTunes card? (It was a Coldplay song — you like them, Mom.)

Lily

March 1/ Subject: so uncomfortable

Mom, tonight my host mother asked me how things are going with Julia. Talk about a *touchy* subject. Though she doesn't talk too much, I don't think there's a huge problem between Julia and me. But honestly, Mom, she really *does not* want to go out with me and help me *discover* Rome. We are sweet to each other in passing (how was your day — fine. Good night — sweet dreams. Could you grab me an umbrella — sure.) But she just wants to stay home or hang at her friends.

What am I supposed to do about *that*?

Your bambina, Lily

Date: March 1
Subject: mothers hey?

I guess I see your point. But I also know you are mature enough to see that sometimes politeness needs to come before independence, so that you are not snubbing them by setting off on your own continually.

It's March! You've been a Canadian in Italy for more than a month. Can you believe it is still snowing here? But it was always this way when you used to shovel Mrs. B's walks — March had all the snow.

Xoxo, Mom

Date: March 8
Subject: Oh dear — Zoë

Saw an early spring robin in the lilac bush. The first one is supposed to be lucky.

I'm going to Vancouver this weekend to see Zoë. She's getting incredibly stressed about completing her grad project for her degree. She long ago decided to do a mural on the wall, which of course she can't start until the "walls" for the show go up a few days before the event. No one could talk her out of it. I'm staying at a hotel on Granville Island, and I suggested she come and have a sleepover with me. It will be good for her. For me, too. I miss my girls.

love, Mom

Date: March 17
Subject: love languages

I hope you and Zoë didn't eat much all day, and then, at night, you got some fancy dessert with chocolate and ice cream to share, and went to a sweet movie, and were all warm in those nice big, clean hotel beds. I love hotels.

I want to get a gift for my host mom because she had surgery on her ankle, but I don't know what she would appreciate. I'm trying to figure out her love languages.

Mom, I discovered the best place to sunbathe on this island in the middle of the river — Isola Tiberina. There's this pretty hospital and when you walk down the steps next to the hospital, you get to an area where people sit around. It gets nice and warm, and you can always hear the water flowing. I started reading Dante's Inferno there today...

Tell me the truth. Is Zoë okay?

Love, Lily

Date: March 20
Subject: a surprising life

Zoë's had better days. I'm sure the mural will be amazing, but it's a big challenge that she's set for herself — so stressful.

Yes, figuring out your host's love languages would help. I know it must be hard living with strangers. I admire you for it. All the same, what a surprising life you are living. Don't let it start to feel too *day in, day out.* Keep trying to capture the uniqueness of the experience you are having, whatever that might be.

I've bought a language CD; let me try my Italian out on you. *Come sta?* Lily. *Cosa si puo fare last weekend?*

Buonasera, Mom

Date: April 5
Subject: Now Who's the Email Queen?

I'm so tired of seeing American girls walking around this city in beautifully put-together outfits when I'm just clumping my way around with messy hair and dirty shoes and a lumpy hoodie, wishing I had that clean, creative look every girl but me has. Then sometimes I just stop dead in my tracks and wonder if it even matters, if I'd be happier just to go home, climb in bed and fill my already cluttered head with more teachings of Nietzsche.

I met two sweet girls yesterday though, in a park after my Italian lesson. It was this unbelievably beautiful garden and they were reading Plato in French, so I took a few pictures of them and listened for a while, then we went for drinks at a cafe in Trastevere. I managed all the conversation in Italian.

There are so many cute boys at my school, but the cute ones never talk to me. I would probably be disappointed if they did. There's one boy in the fifth year named Matteo but he's *so* strange. Here's the story of him: The first time we met, he seemed happy that I had read *The Unbearable Lightness of Being*, but his English wasn't good enough for us to talk. I always see him saying things, accompanied by these major hand gestures, that seem so interesting to his friends (always boys) who are either listening intently or laughing a lot. I tried to talk to him in the hallway, but he responded minimally and was inching away from me the whole time. So I guess he's either shy with girls or he's gay.

Then there's a boy in the second year who is soooooo cute, but I've never talked to him. He seems cool to me, probably because he won't even glance in my direction.

So how do I get this boy to notice me, momma? Honestly it would be easy if I saw him alone somewhere — I would just go up and talk to him. But I'm not going to chase him down the hallway... Okay, this is ridiculous; he's never even looked at me once.

So there you have it! There's cute boys here, but either I'm not cute enough for them or they're not brave/nice/straight enough for me. So it is just me, here in Rome.

Lily (haha, this is the longest email in my life, Email Queen)

Date: April 3
Subject: what of Italian boys

Why don't you get Julia to recommend a salon and let them trim your hair so that it is even and blunt — that was one of the best cuts you ever had — you know like in the photo with Santa I keep on my dresser. Now that you aren't nine, it would look dramatic on you. It might encourage Zoë to get rid of what are now looking like totally unmanageable dreadlocks.

Be brave. Comb your hair. Throw your shoulders back and go right up to that boy and ask him a question. Try out your Italian. See if he answers.

...and Lily, photos?

love you, Mom

Date: April 11
Subject: Ho amato Napoli.

Mom, my host family took me to Napoli, which is a lot scarier than Rome, though we saw a magnificent castle and a city that was once covered by earth when Vesuvius erupted.

One of my favourite moments was Saturday night. Julia and I were sharing a room, and we got home late from dinner and brought some chairs onto the balcony where we could see a fat full moon and just talked.

I can't believe I never thought to ask Zoë whether she knows what a total hippie she is since going to art school and living in Vancouver. I mean her heart is just the heart of a girl named Zoë, so she can be whoever she wants. But I think we have to admit that if someone were to list the characteristics of your typical hippie... they'd hit that list right on Zoë's messy dreadlocked head.

Love you, Lily

Date: April 18
Subject: Country Mouse

This weekend, we went to a country house for Easter weekend. The countryside was all rolling hills, with tiny houses and orchards in the valleys and little towns built on the peaks. Friday afternoon, we ate lunch (paninis and strawberries and honey), and I read in the sun (it was the sunniest day) and then walked to town along the tiny streets with the sleeping cats and hanging laundry until I found, at the end of the street, once you pass under the archway, a sunny, bright terrace that looked out over the country, the train tracks, a lake, and the setting sun. I sat there for a few hours until the sky was purple and eventually found my way home for dinner.

Sunday, Julia came on the train, and the Easter celebration was more about opening our chocolate eggs than eating a big meal. Well... because every meal is pretty extravagant in Italy, it's hard to take it much further on holidays.

My host mother put lilacs on the table and when I smelled them, I got a pretty sharp stab of homesickness. Yes, I still get those — reassurance that I'll be happy to come home.

Flip side, family!

Love, Lily

Date: April 18
Subject: Ah Lilacs

Thank you, Lily, for the photos — at last. You look different over there in the busy street — you look Italian. And your hair is longer, and is it possible that you look more worldly? I love the flower boxes. It makes me want to put mine in boxes this year instead of round planters. Silly.

You have lilacs on the table there when we don't even have an open leaf bud here. The frothy pink Nanking cherry flowers have yet to blossom. But the sun is shining, the tulip leaves are up, and people are raking still-brown grass and digging in the dirt just to be outside. I'm going to plant sweet peas here today for that very reason.

I am not lonely per se, but I am lonely for you. I hope our trip comes up rapidly.

Love lots, Mom (send more photos — they did capture what it is that you were afraid would be missing)

Date: April 21
Subject: non ti preoccupare

Man, it really sucks when people don't respond to my emails for a long time. Most friends don't write me unless I write them. It's not a huge tragedy. I like how this exchange thing involves all this isolation.

As for Julia, I ask her to come along with me sometimes now, and she asks me, but it's just a courtesy. I open up about feelings and thoughts more than she does, though she's a good listener even if she doesn't understand. We're casual enough now, so that's cool.

love, lily

Date: April 22
Subject: still light at almost 9 p.m.

Hey Lily, could you tell how excited we were to get your call? The photography festival sounded amazing. I wonder if there will be anything special on when we are there.

I put in loads of sweet peas. I love sweet peas. Then I started to clean up the old plants, sticks, leaves, and pine cones from the garden. It was cool outside and I had a winter jacket on, but I was enjoying it. Like most gardeners, I do it not as much for the brief (in this country) results, as for the relaxing pleasure I get from the work. It's hard to explain, because it doesn't seem very cerebral or creative, but playing in the garden does feel, in the same way that writing does, like "a time away from time." That is a quote from a book I bought for you called, "Letters to a Young Artist," by Julia Cameron.

After I scanned the book, I thought Zoë would like it more than you. But I read sections to Zoë, and she said it wasn't the right time for her to read about how to succeed when she is so deeply involved in working hard at just that. I'll bring it for you.

Love, Mom

Date: April 23
Subject: Are you kidding?

This is Rome we're talking about, mom. There will be about ten thousand art shows on. Maybe the Leonardo Da Vinci exhibit will still be here.

I totally understand how gardening must feel good. Totally.

Calling Zoë was definitely the best way I could've spent my Saturday night. I was so happy to talk to her, like, so happy. We talked our heads off — well, Zoë more than me. I can't wait to see her. I love her so much. Thanks for making us. You're my favourite mom.

Lily

Date: April 23
Subject: MOM STOP

Oh, my god. I talked to Hudson and he told me you are arranging for some tour when you are here. What the heck, mom? I want to show you the Rome I know from wandering around here all this time. No one wants to go on some lame tour where we have to wear name tags and listen to some bossy person with a British accent, who waves a flag to get our attention. And, mom, is Zoë okay? Hudson said she wasn't exactly herself, in some *boy way* of talking where he wouldn't really explain what he meant.

Lily

Date: April 24
Subject: it'll be fine/no name tags

Honey, you almost had me convinced, but Dad and I talked, and first and foremost, we do want to see the Rome you know shown to us by you, but we also want to have a short tour (four hours) of some of the sites with an English-speaking guide to give us some of the history. For instance, did you know that the people in Trastevere claim to be the only true Romans now or that the Santa Maria Church may be one of the oldest in Rome, and on the day of Christ's birth, a spring of olive oil was said to flow from it into the Tiber River? Or that the Coliseum is now less than half its original size and the Roman appetite for gala massacres led to the extinction of the lions and elephants from North Africa?

Or how about this — some of Michelangelo's fantastic figures on the Sistine Chapel ceiling had pants painted on them after his death, by order of some crazy ruler, Pius the IV? And did you know that if you throw a coin into the

Fontana Di Trevi, it will bring you good luck and ensure your return to Rome — and that the coins are collected and go to the Red Cross? Or that the fountain, dating from 19 BC, is fed from an aqueduct 20 km east of the city?

Be patient, Lily, and recognize that this tour won't take away from what you can show us. You'll be able to show off to the guide and chatter in Italian with him about your silly family. Okay?

love, Mom

Date: April 24
Subject: I did know most of that stuff.

But okay. Lily

Date: April 25
Subject: Cosmic Puppets

Mom, you didn't answer me about Zoë. Don't "not tell me" things because I'm here. I got a cold somehow this weekend, but I made some hot water with lemon and honey. Julia came home and we talked more than usual. She even read me a few pages out of the copy of *Lolita* I bought her for her birthday. We're going to make paninis and watch a movie in Italian. This is all positive, because we didn't talk much this weekend in the country.

Friday was a holiday here so we went to their country place which is close to the Adriatic Sea. On Monday, at about the time everyone in Calgary was waking up to go to school, I was lying on a long strip of soft sand with the blue sea ahead of me and the hot, sunny sky above. I read *The Cosmic Puppets* by Philip K. Dick. I totally hate science fiction.

I had intense dreams last night. I feel so scared to leave Italy, but also sort of scared in general. Well, i feel better now. There's no wrong way to live, right?

love lily

Date: April 27
Subject: Ah Bunny

What sort of sick are you? Throat? Snotty nose? Fever? Are you taking Vitamin C and sleeping?

I didn't want to worry you, but I'll tell you now that Zoë lost days and days of sleep prior to her grad show and threw herself totally out of sorts — totally. It wasn't pretty. Anxiety can play havoc with one's sense of self. Of course, she made incredible art but is just now getting back on track.

Love, your stressed out mom

Date: April 28
Subject: eccitata

Zoë's okay now though, right? Me — I'm throat nose sick, but my host father is a doctor so the slightest thing gets treated like a huge emergency. It's really funny. The other day i came home with blisters on my feet, and we all sat down in the bathroom and he put on his glasses and was all "let's see what we have here..." or that would be "ora vediamo cosa ce..."

Knowing you guys are coming soon, I can't express how excited I am! Like, how lucky am I that I get to do a holiday WITHIN my immersion program.

Did you know that Italians consider excitement to be the same as agitation (=agitata)... They consider excitement negative. I'm going to the Lou Reed photo show tonight! Sooo agitated!

Love Lily

Date: May 9
Subject: take a deep breath before you read this

Okay, Lily, relax and don't worry when you read this — you and I have to work together in a really calm way. It will be fine. I just got an email from the immersion program here in Canada saying that they have heard from the Italy office that we are taking you travelling for 14 days and that would be a big problem with your missing school. Don't worry.

I don't know how it will play out, but once again, "more bees with honey" is the way to go here. I wrote this email to assure them.

> Dear Ms. _____, I must apologize for taking so long to return your email. I have been in Vancouver as my eldest daughter was graduating from the Emily Carr School of Art and Design there. It was her gradation that led us to plan to take her to Italy even before we knew that was the country that her sister, Lily, would have her immersion experience in.
>
> I understand your concerns and I can assure you Lily will not miss 14 days of school. The first part of our trip is in Rome and we have told her she should plan to attend school every day while we are busy seeing the city that she is familiar with. At the very most, she will miss seven days. She has spoken to her teachers about this, and there doesn't seem to be an issue at all.
>
> With respect,

I can just feel you fuming, Lily, but listen to me — you may have to attend school those first four days in Rome. Let's do the honey thing. Dad says to tell you to hush up about not going to school while we're there AND that going may be the small sacrifice you make for us to leave Rome free of hassle. Whatever you do — do not blow your top.

Zoë is definitely better. We were all holding our breaths waiting for her to finish her mural in time and come back to earth, but she did it and came home from Vancouver to sort herself out. We can't wait to see you.

Love, Mommy

Date: May 10
Subject: Can't Be Calm!!

Okay I'm sorry but the other immersion students in Rome have taken trips. And there's **no way** I'll want to go to school those days while you are in Rome. Seriously, I learn way more Italian outside of school, meeting people and having conversations.

You do the honey thing and I'll try to stay calm, but I'm **not** going to school. I'm just not. I'm really, really, really not. I won't.

ps. Please bring me Crest toothpaste (vanilla), Lily

Date: May 11
Subject: crush

Mom, on second thought, I might not mind going to school one or two of those days. My Italian is getting so good I can totally understand my philosophy teacher now. And remember that boy I told you about who never looks at me and who I'm afraid to talk to? Well, a week ago i

115

told him about this dream i had with him in it (I was really lame about it and he seemed totally weirded out), but today I took him and two other boys in his class to see this gallery near the school. It turned out to be closed but i got to talk to him and prove that I'm not insane! Ah he's so cute. I'm all crushing. See you SO soon. Ciao momma.

Post Italy visit

Date: June 1
Subject: Hey Lily, would you like to read the email I sent to family and friends about our trip?

Salute,

Wow — 14 days in Italy with two adults and four sort-of adults! The night Hudson and Zoë got lost in Venice amongst the winding alleyways and moonlit canals after 2 a.m. was almost more than my Canadian heart could take. Of course, the next night poor Cole ended up sleeping on the sidewalk after hitting some clubs on his own, because we'd mistakenly locked him out of our "apartment" separated from the main hotel and managed to sleep through him tossing rocks onto our third storey windowsill.

Our first day, Lily toured us through the streets of her neighbourhood. It was amazing to hear Italian roll off her lips. We dined on magnificent pizza, accompanied by a little dish of fresh basil, in an outdoor cafe while she calmly instructed us in useful phrases. By the thirteenth night, we were discussing the cheese and bread–free diet we'd go on at home and shouting like pushy Americans/Canadians, "Lily, ask if the fish is fried. Lily, ask if the tip is included. Lily, tell them the polenta sucks."

By Florence, the boys were starting the day with double espressos and drinking them to keep going after our ten-thirty dinners. It was there that they tried fried beef brains. I chose our Florence hotel for its charming location. It was set in the most picturesque meadow amongst the Tuscan hills. (Zoë commented that she now understood the settings the authors of the fairytales of her childhood were describing.) Our almost-adult kids chased fireflies and we listened to nightingales sing in the dark.

I believe the highlight was a bike ride Zoë, Cole, and Hudson took in Tuscany (through rolling fields — not paths, just fields) while Will, Lily, and I learned to make ravioli in a Tuscan farmhouse. Then we all dined together on a homemade meal — rich potato frittata, creamy risotto, crisp asparagus pizza, the ravioli we'd made, and fresh strawberries and cream.

Afterwards we demanded that our little translator, Lily, locate the movie The Da Vinci Code which we believed was playing in English somewhere in Florence. "Come on, Lily, ask someone else. Ask that guy — he looks smart. Okay, ask that Polizzia officer." No go, though — only dubbed movies in Firenze. Zoë, though the oldest, was happy to hang with us, but Lily, Cole, and Hudson seldom missed a chance to at least search for nightclubs. It's a different world where 16-year-old Lily can order cuba libres and vino rosso — but one with a healthier attitude, I'm sure.

Cinque Terra is where we wanted to stay forever. Here we swam in the Mediterranean, basked/burned in the sun, hiked the Via dell'Amore — lover's lane — from one of the five little mountain towns to the next, and dined on the best fried calamari. If you ever go to Italy, go to Cinque Terra, stay at the Spiaggia Hotel in Monterosso (overlooking the street and the sea), and drink lots of complementary wine with the proprietor (he'll insist).

Our last stop was Venice. We'd just finished a dinner in the piazza outside our apartment and were talking about how easy it would be to get completely lost there. We wandered around together until we discovered an Italian outdoor karaoke bar and, in the excitement, lost track of each other in pairs. Will and I found our way *home* first, then Cole and Lily, but Zoë and Hudson were headed inland caught up in a philosophical discussion, and while trying to unravel the mysteries of the universe, they got lost for hours amongst the winding alleys, piazzas (squares with four exits), bridges, and waterways. (We only have one cellphone here — Will's Blackberry — so that was no help.) We formed a search party and hours after we parted, Will and Cole found them on the Rialto Bridge looking sheepish and relieved.

On our last Venetian day, we found the Palazzo Grassi which was featuring a display of modern art — so thrilling for Zoë as she'd recently studied some of the featured artists' works, Gerhard Richter, Jeff Wall, Jeff Koons, Mark Rothko, and Damien Hirst.

Lily was growing melancholy — she was happy being her *Calgary self* with us and was a bit nervous about returning to being her *Rome self*, though she wanted to relish her last month in Rome. We hugged and kissed, and kissed and hugged Lily goodbye — she is very confident travelling now and was finding her way back to Rome alone. Leaving Venice by water taxi at sunrise with the sea mist just lifting over the ancient architecture was so beautiful it prompted Hudson to take his second photo of the trip (the first was of an Italian girl on a train).

And so we're home, taking a break from cheese, vowing to walk much more, and missing the streets filled with people, the cafes, the scooters, the kissing of Italians, and, of course, Lily.

Ciao

Date: June 6
Subject: Problem with Julia

I am trying to work this out. There are a lot of understandable reasons why Julia doesn't like me being around: I arrived when she arrived home from Brazil, and instead of getting back to her regular life, she had to get used to a new person in the house, and she's never had a sister. My Italian is probably misinterpreted sometimes as being pushy because I haven't mastered the right intonation yet, and I'm just different than her. Today and yesterday, I was being super, super nice, and, of course, when I'm nicer, she's nicer.

Please don't count the days I have left. I can't even describe the inner conflict I have about leaving. Let's just say I'll be ready when the day comes but not **one** second before.

Tonight I went to a party at a classmate's house. Or, more accurately, ON his house, on the rooftop terrace. I think one of the guys likes me but is too afraid to do anything about it. I wish he would.

You better wean my brothers off their coffee addictions.

Lily

Date: June 8
Subject: Why is nothing ever good when you're in the middle of it?

So, mom, school here is over. Which is awesome, but what am I going to do with all the time? I guess I'll just read in gardens. I wish a lot of things. Like for the future. I have so many plans.

Mom, I'm so homesick... that's the gosh-darned truth. I feel dumb. Why is nothing ever good when you're in the middle of it? Before I came here, I had all these little fantasies of what it would be like, and it wasn't like that at all, although it was amazing in other ways that I didn't predict. But with home, it's different, because I know exactly what I'm coming back to, though I'm still working it up to be more magical than it will feel.

I want to go to Montreal after I'm finished high school and take some film and photo classes, and get a part-time job and a cheap, cheap apartment. All I require for this apartment is that it have a terrace. Lily

Date: June 13
Subject: I need to vent

Mom I miss *you* being my mom sooooooo much. It is so difficult with my host mom sometimes. Okay, so there was this stupid immersion program get-together the other day in the basement of a community hall (so you can imagine how badly I wanted to leave the second we got there — another thing you and I have in common, mom: intolerance for life-sucking spaces). The idea was for me and the other four girls who were placed in Rome to talk about our impressions of the program in front of this big group of Roman kids who are about to do immersion programs all over the world.

I spoke first to get it over with, but I didn't make any sense at all because I was too nervous to think straight and have good Italian. So we all spoke and then they called everyone's host families up to speak. My host mom talked for like seven minutes! She told everyone — all these Italian kids, all their parents, all the other host families, and all the volunteers — about how hard it was for all of us to adjust at the beginning, because Julia had just got back from her exchange to Brazil. She made it sound like I was homesick and distraught, but with the help of the wonderful volunteers, they managed to overcome all that inconvenience I caused. I was just standing there in awe rubbing my forehead as she went on and on and on, making everyone think I was some kind of disaster, maybe even a precautionary tale to all the young students about to embark. After all that, when we were leaving, she told me I'd got fatter in the time I've been here.

It's just so hard sometimes, mom. This morning I came into the kitchen with a knife to put in the dishwasher and saw that the dishes in there were clean. I said, these are clean? and she said yes, so I put the knife down on the counter and was about to empty the dishwasher and she said, you could also empty it, you know. I was JUST about to do that but I don't know how to say, I was just about to do that, so I had to just say si, like a servant.

Well, I'll be gone soon. Missing you, Lily

Date: June 13
Subject: oh Lily baby

If ever there were a time to stay calm and try your hardest to get along, this would be it.

You'll be back here in your own bed, having breakfast on our deck (sort of a terrace), and emptying our dishwasher soon. I have to think that you are with good people there, but five months has been a long time for all of you, especially with the language barrier. Hopefully you can leave with fond memories, and you'll have succeeded at what so many kids your age would never attempt.

Love you Sweetie Pie, Mom

P.S. Cole says I should not take you so seriously and you are probably being way oversensitive. Honey, who knows what was really going on?

Love More, Mom

Date: June 13
Subject: I've got the leaving here blues

Ha ha, well Cole's partly right. I've discovered that my host mom makes more of an effort to talk and be nice to me when I've given her space. Listen, don't worry. Things are tranquil enough.

It went so fast. Sometimes I'm just praying that the time will go by faster, but the closer it gets, the less I think about Calgary and more about what I'll miss. The smell of fresh basil on pizza, the motorinos that are so comfy to lie on when you're just hanging around in the street, the fact that people just hang around in the street...

But guess what, mom?! A friend of my host brother's, who works at the bar by my house, said they want to do a show of my photos! So I'm going to have that going on for my last week here. Isn't that sweet?

Lily

Date: June 14
Subject: You'd be proud of your non-Italian mother

Wish like crazy that I could see your photo show. Cole and I are studying the art of real Italian pizza making. The owner of my favourite Italian deli here in Calgary gave me instructions on how to make it authentic, though I insulted him by asking if he watched The Sopranos. He ranted about how it gives Italians a bad reputation — obviously a soft spot. So the secret (shshshh) is to be careful with the sauce (not very much at all), use real mozzarella, of course — the bocconcini that we ate in Italy — add roasted peppers, and top with fresh parmesan. Another tip: brush olive oil and salt on the thinly rolled crust. Oh yeah — can't forget the fresh basil on top. He said that you should come by to converse in Italian with him. (Don't mention The Sopranos.)

Zoë is in Vancouver painting a mural for the American TV drama The L Word, the show about cool lesbian women. Crazy, hey? They hired her after someone from the show saw the mural she did for her graduation at Emily Carr. So something wonderful from the over-the-top stress.

love, trying to be sort-of-an-Italian mother, Mom

Date: June 19
Subject: Leaving here blues — maybe not blue — sort of aqua

Last night I went to this skateboarding video premiere and met a bunch of really funny skateboard boys. Then I went to that bar to get plans down for the photo show I'm doing there, before coming home and calling Daniel (my sorta boyfriend at home). I was so happy when I went to bed that I had to listen to my iPod just so I could stop thinking about how happy I was and be able to sleep.

Lily

Date: June 19
Subject: Melancholy

It's funny, Lily, having you coming home, and being all excited about that — and having Cole leaving for New Zealand, and being a little sad about that. He's been sick so isn't quite as chipper as he should be. Hudson is happier these days though. Life is so funny, hey? I want everyone to be happy, but that often means they are off on an adventure and going away.

kisses and good night, Mommy

Date: June 19
Subject: L-I to the F-E, I know you get shit on but you'll always have me.

You're so right — life is hilarious. I like a boy here. Isn't that a riot? In the month before leaving Calgary, I got kind of numb and wanted to stay and leave pretty equally, and spent more time with Daniel. Now in this last month in Rome, the exact same thing is happening. (Stay calm, mom.)

Well not EXACT, because I know more or less what I'm coming home to, but I don't know when I'll return to Rome (difficult thing), and this boy here is really sweet.

love you, Lily

Date: June 20
Subject: mom to the LMR

Oh, you are a last minute romantic, aren't you? Well, have fun, but don't get too serious because I don't know when you are going back to Rome either. HOW OLD IS HE? Don't tell me a *young* 21? I don't buy that.

Remember how we put stickers with your name on all your processions that could be stolen. We didn't put a sticker on your innocence so don't lose it! Seriously — love, Mom

Date: June 21
Subject: ho fatto una brutta spesa

You're weird.

I met him in February and we hung out a couple of times and then i ran into him again recently and we could actually talk to each other because I know Italian now! He is 21. But a normal 21, not a young 21. Believe me, that's a good thing. He's very mature and nice and not some creep who's into me because I'm younger. Girls in Italy always go out with older guys. Honest. But yeah, don't worry; we mostly just hang out.

Lily

ps. oh yeah, i dreamed last night that I had to go grocery shopping here for my host mom, but i brought the food back to our Calgary home and told you in Italian that I had done a bad job. "Ho fatto una brutta spesa." My dreams are crazy.

(what's LMR? Learned Mothers against Reproduction? License to Maintain and Reassure?)

Date: June 21
Subject: Re: mom to the LMR

LMR — last minute romantic

I'm not weird. Just remember — what's normal there isn't here. Here 21-year-olds DO NOT date 16-year-olds. Sorry, Lily, he's an adult. You're not. End of story.

love, Mom

Date: June 21
Subject: you are DEFINITELY kind of weird

But in a really hilarious, lovable way. Wow, perfect name for the photo show — Last Minute Romantic — thanks.

Lily

Date: June 21
Subject: Re: mom to the LMR

But you are not going to date him, right, Lily? Can you just tell me that you won't?

Parenting from here is hard. I don't want to use our emails like a "Dear Diary," but I will tell you that I feel out of sorts right now, too. Poor Cole is sick — bad, bad sore throat and a nasty infection in his mouth. He took himself off his allergy medicine after four years, scorched his mouth on over-heated pizza, and ate ridiculously hot peppers on a dare. No kissing any girls goodbye for him.

I don't know if I can put my finger on how I am "out of sorts" — just thinking about you coming home and Cole leaving.

Love, Mom

Date: June 24
Subject: Boo hoo hoo

Mommy, i wrote an email to all of my closest friends two days ago and only one of them wrote back. I feel so **un**missed.

They're probably having some insanely awesome summer over there and they don't even have time to remember their old friend Lily. Is poor Cole better?

Ciao

Date: June 24
Subject: stiff upper lip

Honey, students still have exams this week. It's just starting to feel like summer.

It is one of those Junes where it rains every day — so it's green and lush like spring, not hot like summer. I'm dusting and vacuuming your room and washing your sheets and there is an air here of anticipation of your return — believe me.

Love you so much, my old friend Lily. Love you to the moon. Mom

Date: June 24
Subject: not the moon

No, swear not by the moon! The inconstant moon that monthly changes with its circular orb!

Wow i think that's almost exactly what Juliet says....

Lily

Date: June 25
Subject: Exactly

Exactly, I love you no matter how inconstant you are.

Speaking of seasons — Cole is packed for winter in New Zealand. He'll fly away from here — solo — with an almost healed mouth, in two days...

Savour your last week in Rome.

Ti Amo, Mom

Date: June 28
Subject: Whew! Almost home.

hey dad and mom,

Hung out with friends last night, but tonight I need to be alone. I'm going to go watch the sunset by Piazza Venezia. I have enough things to do now because I'm doing my last times.

love you! bye.

Date: July 2
Subject: waiting hard to hear from Cole

Still haven't heard from Cole since he got on the plane to New Zealand five days ago, which is really upsetting me. It is hard to have him act like Chris McCandless when he has parents as *supportive*, shall we say, as we've been. What with that, I can hardly wait to have you home and here.

Thank your hosts profusely. Love mom.

Date: July 3
Subject: heartbroken

Now who's chris mccandless? Have I been away so long that I'm forgetting people you would assume I know? oh wait, no, I remember Chris McCandless. He was that adventure guy who died in the abandoned bus in Alaska. The book is Into the Wilds, right?

Cole will get in touch but yeah, you're right — you and dad are really the wrecking ball to all of our outlaw runaway fantasies. Why couldn't you jerks go and be crack addicts or religious fanatics so we could have excuses to live on the wide open road?

Tonight will be my last night in Rome. I'm realizing a lot of truths about my time here. I want to be *mad* at Rome because being mad at it is emotionally easier than being heartbroken to leave it, which, in all actuality, I am.

After dinner, I'll walk around Trastevere and go up to Gianicolo to look over the city. It's better to say goodbye to all of it at once.

Try not to worry about Cole, Mom.

Lily

Chapter 13

Lost Down Under

Okay Mom, you have to make us all badass, so we can turn your book into a movie script. You can quote me saying whatever. Just make it good.

– Cole, in film school

On the days when I'm having mild panic attacks over the exploits of my kids, I like to consider those mothers who have nine or ten children — or that one on television with nineteen. I wonder what the heck they were thinking. Some people might surmise that those mothers worry less because there's only so much one person can worry. But worry, like love, multiplies; it doesn't max out. Often in the morning, I lie in bed and take a tally of my four kids, rating how fervently I need to worry about them on a given day.

Zoë, I'll say to myself, no worries with her today. Next, Cole — he seems to be having trouble choosing a path and that girl messed with his heart. Some worries there. Okay — Hudson. Well, Hudson worries, philosophizes, and ruminates enough on his own. Of course, that's another thing to worry about. And then

Lily: Lily is in a good space, I'll decide, so no worrying necessary. Other days, the boys will be happy and in the clear, but Zoë will be frustrated with her crowded house of roommates and frantic over a grad school application, and Lily will tell me she had a horrible night's sleep and she feels like she doesn't have any good friends and, by the way, why do I think she hasn't had one serious boyfriend — and so on.

I think mothers of nineteen kids do the same kind of tally; it just keeps them in bed longer in the morning or awake further into the night. Obviously I had worried about Cole plenty, but he moved up to the numero uno spot when he decided to travel alone, circling halfway around the globe, to New Zealand. It didn't help that I was still recovering from the dramatics of his US trip. Still, I worried about Cole in a different way than I did the others. I worried about him breaking more bones snowboarding, skateboarding, or wakeboarding. I worried about him partying too hard and even exercising too much, but I didn't worry about Cole worrying. Though his ideas could be all over the map, like many young adults with still maturing frontal lobes, when Cole did latch onto a plan, he attacked it with resolve. He has been described as having the gift of the gab, the ability to persuade others to follow his lead or buy into his ideas. Sometimes I've found myself worrying about those he's so easily persuaded.

When Cole was working as a lift operator, we packed the family into the van and drove twelve hours to take a short winter ski holiday in Whistler. We met Cole's lanky Quebecois roommates, stocked their fridge with healthy food, and let our son sleep in our hotel — piled up in a bed with his contented siblings. He told us that at staff meetings, the employers would remind the kids to eat fruit or take vitamin C. It was a comfort during our visit to see that there were adults taking some responsibility for the hundreds of kids, like Cole, working on the mountain. The resort had a website that I was able to get on that provided the rules and regulations for the resort staff as well as notice of upcoming staff meetings and the occasional after-hours party the supervisors organized. I bet I wasn't the only mom who bookmarked that site to try to surmise what was happening with my kid so far away. When Cole first proposed his six-month trip to New Zealand, I wanted just such a website. Twenty-year-olds travelling alone in New Zealand, it would say, must abide by these safety rules. I told people at the time that, of any of my kids, I felt most comfortable with Cole crisscrossing that distant country from Queenstown to the Marlborough Sounds alone, and I added that, of any country, New Zealand felt the safest. That was before Will turned on the movie Wolf Creek late one night and I made the mistake of watching a deranged killer in Australia's outback (which is only 1,490 km from New Zealand) beguiling, drugging and torturing a group of young foreign travellers. I never told my curious friends the thoughts that would torture me at four in the morning during those times when I hadn't heard from Cole for over a week and imagined him hitchhiking God knows where.

Cole purchased a pay-as-you-go cellphone with erratic service so he could stay in touch with fellow travellers, snowboard buddies, and potential employers. Back then, my kids were just starting to use text messages, tapping away to each other at breakneck speeds. Mobile service plans that provided "unlimited texting" for a flat fee facilitated the new method of communication. I had yet to realize the benefits of texting myself, though a few months later I would be insisting to other moms that it was the preeminent way to communicate and get a quick response from your kids — sons, in particular. Still, international texting wasn't part of Cole's or my phone plans.

It was late one rainy afternoon, just as dusk was settling in Calgary, that Cole called home from Down Under, amazed that he had cell service because, he said, he was on the north island in the middle of nowhere trying to hitch a ride back south for a job interview. I could hear the echo of his footsteps along the road. Feeling the great distance between us and still recovering from the psycho killer flick, I pleaded with him to please stop hitchhiking, telling him I'd lend him money to cover his bus fare. "You have to chill out, Mom," he said. "Everyone hitchhikes in New Zealand. It's not like at home. It's different here; there are lots of places buses just don't go." Cole was chatty, which was unusual, because, despite his talkative nature in person, he isn't a phone talker, much like the rest of the males in our family. He seemed lonely for me or family, or just company, as was I, that dreary day. I could hear the wind over the phone as he told me about the ridiculous distance he was trying to cover in an attempt to get to a job interview at Treble Cone near Wanaka, miles and miles away. I don't know if it was dark where he was, but I imagined a gray sky overhead as he asked, in a voice rising above the wind, how everyone was doing. Was Hudson liking university (not particularly), had I heard from Zoë lately (no, but I decided right then to call her the next day), what about Lily, did she like being the only kid at home (definitely not), and Dad, how was Dad? He started to tell me about the group of travellers he'd lived with and how New Zealanders eat pie, not just fruit pie but every type of pie: lamb pie, bacon pie, crocodile pie, emu pie... and right then, we lost the connection. Cole, I called into the phone, Cole... I imagined him doing the same, Mom? Mom?

I called one friend after another to go for a therapeutic walk, but no one was home. I called Will and Lily, but got their voicemails. I tried hard to think of all the enthusiastic praise Cole had for New Zealand: how beautiful it was, how the people were as friendly as everyone has always said, how the place was full of Canadians like him travelling and snowboarding and eating pie. Crocodile pie? I tried to imagine one of those friendly, pie-eating people picking him up and fulfilling his need to chat. But, of course, all I could think of was Cole standing on the highway having lost the connection to home.

It reminded me of the time we lost him when he was just a little boy. I honestly try to never think of it, but the tale has become folklore, not just in our household, but on our street amongst friends and neighbours. It had been a spring night, not dreary at all, but rather clear and full of the promise of summer.

We'd eaten supper later than I realized, though it was still light out. When I told six-year-old Cole that he could take his tiny two-wheel bike and go meet his friends a few houses up the street, I was under the impression that it was far earlier. There are other excuses I always feel I have to make — I was doing laundry and bathing the two youngest, there was a lot of noise in the house, sounds were being muffled.

Suddenly the light coming into the house shifted from daylight to dusk, and I was alarmed to realize it was past eight and Cole hadn't come in. His six-year-old friends would have been on their way to bed. As calmly as possible, I asked Zoë, Hudson, and even little Lily if they'd seen him and then shouted his name from the front steps before calling his friends' homes to no avail. My manner changed as dramatically as the light had shifted from day to twilight. I was frantic as I screamed at the children to help me, and then left them alone to race to the car and circle the nearest blocks, before phoning my sister and asking her if she thought I should call the police. Two of Cole's friend's mothers phoned back to see if I'd found him. My heart was beating against my chest. One mother offered to come over, and another said she'd go out looking.

I dialed 911. The operator asked me to describe his clothing. I didn't know what t-shirt he had on and suddenly pictured myself in a day or two, in between making sandwiches for the search parties, still trying to figure that out. Panic was giving way to hysteria, and the 911 operator began to treat me like a woman on the edge. She told me to stay in the house until the police arrived, and, in a strained voice, I refused. "I have to find my kid," I said. "I have to go find him." The following day, I complained about the tone of voice she used, but later I could see that it was necessary for her to be firm and strict, as if I was a child, and she had to be certain her directions were going to be followed. "You have to be there in case he comes home. You have to be there to talk to the police. Do you understand me?"

Downstairs, my neighbour was reading Goodnight Moon to my other kids, keeping them away from the situation. My panic amplified as the calm words carried up the stairs. Goodnight, cow jumping over the moon. Goodnight, light and the red balloon. I felt I was physically holding my head onto my shoulders with one raised arm, still calling his name inside the house, when the police arrived. Rushing outside to meet the patrol cars, I was shocked to see the street filled with people, cars, and even bicycles. Without being asked, my neighbours had organized a search. People were knocking on doors. Motorists and bicyclists were being sent further afield. The description of a six-year-old blond boy in a jean jacket was being given to all who passed by. I was too terrified then to be impressed with the way people had taken charge and organized the search.

The story gets muddled when I mention the dream. Still, it was part of the incident and an overriding source of my fear. The night before, I had been jolted awake after dreaming of a boy lying down, accompanied by a feeling of dread. I hadn't mentioned my nightmare to Will, deciding it was too disturbing to talk about, but I had recalled it that afternoon and wondered what it meant and why it had to blemish an otherwise pleasant day. The cops arrived and told me, "Don't worry, we'll find your son. Ninety percent of the time these kids are very close to home. Let's start here."

I forced myself to speak up and not be self-conscious. "I had a dream," I said.

"Don't tell me about your dreams," one of the officers barked, turning on his flashlight and sending me into the house. "Look everywhere, places you'd think he'd never go, in every nook and cranny." By then, my sister and her husband had arrived. This was, of course, before cellphones, so she was leaving messages for Will on his and his associate's answering machines. An elderly family friend came to the door to see if she should get my mother for me. The streets were ringing with Cole's name. I never stopped yelling it inside the house.

What world was Cole in right then? Why was he oblivious to all this? Obeying directions, I took one more look in his room and almost collapsed, finding him, curled up tight, hidden under a pillow and a blanket, in the furthest corner beneath his bed. My insides stopped curdling, and tears flowed down my cheeks. I reached for his sleeping body and tried to imagine how many people were now outside hunting for my small son.

In a choked voice, I weakly attempted to find out why he had been hiding but was unsuccessful in getting that information from my groggy boy. The next day, he sheepishly explained that he'd been mad after I told him he had to straighten his room before he could play with his friends, because by the time he rode over to where he'd left them earlier (six-year-old time is a mysterious thing), they'd all gone home. Of course, if I'd realized the hour, he wouldn't have been allowed out at all. The cops briskly told me they were pleased I'd found my son and drove away. The neighbours, who I thanked profusely, said, "You do what you have to do." A few friends came in and mixed drinks to take the edge off. While we waited for Will to return home, we stood on the lawn to inform returning search parties, some consisting of people I'd never spoken to, that all was well. Cole's dad arrived, happily calling out from the van that he'd brought the two of us Chinese food — still without any knowledge of what we'd been through. My mother showed up and said she knew we'd find him.

Aside from deep gratitude, I felt embarrassment for several days, sticking close to home and keeping the blinds down. I assumed that, despite people's assurances otherwise, everyone was talking about the terrible mother who couldn't keep track of her four kids. Cole and I had a few important talks, and more rules were laid down. I recovered, of course. Nothing bad, after all, had happened. Cole had been sleeping under his bed. I vowed to keep better track of the kids and pay more attention to what was going on around me. I imagined bringing them all into bed with me, eight-year-old Zoë bringing her books and Hudson, just four then, amusing us with his belly laughs. At two-years-old (and at three, four, five, and six), Lily's favourite place was our bed anyway. Then, as now, Cole liked to be with friends, so they could visit us in that big comfy bed. The important idea was to keep my kids close for as long as I possibly could. Their dad could bring us what we needed, like a protective bird supplying food for the nest. So how did it happen, not so much later (I mean what's fourteen years?), that I was in Calgary — same house, newer bed — and my second kid, the one who had spurred my desire to keep them all within hand's reach, had left the bed, room, house, city, even country, and gone to the other side of the world, only to call me and lose our connection from a stretch of highway in New Zealand? Where did that rate him on my worry meter that day?

Chapter 14

Text Me, Mr. Tambourine Man

Sure Mom, you can come see my stand-up routine, but no, you are not the source of all my material.

– Hudson

Why am I always surprised by what it is like being the mother of Hudson? My second son is creative, kind, funny, smart — and too often melancholy. A good friend of mine who emigrated from the former Yugoslavia says, "The smart ones are never happy." I went out to Victoria to drive him home from his second year at university. The term had had its up and downs, and Hudson's attention and focus had sometimes ebbed. But I saw first-hand as I watched him pack that amongst his clothes, CDs, and school texts, there were stacks of philosophy books, not required course material but books he'd picked up second-hand for fun. All resistance aside, he was a philosophical and reflective thinker who at age nineteen was attracted to titles like *Our Inner Ape*, *The Essence of Sufism*, and *On Being Free*.

That second year away, he had lived with his aunt and uncle. This had provided him the freedom to conduct his student life, but on weekends, there were cousins to join around the kitchen table. They pulled out a futon for me when I arrived, and I saw that he studied hard for his final two exams, only taking a short break to hang at a pub to say goodbye to friends he described as *good guys, guys he would miss*. He was more mysterious about the girl who inspired him to iron a shirt and shave the night before we left.

Hudson told me convincingly that he was looking forward to our road trip home. "It will be a bonding experience, Mom," he joked. "I know how you mothers like to bond." Yet the mood was sober when we set out. He'd written his last exam that morning, and I heard relief and satisfaction in his voice immediately after. But then there had been a new rush of activity as he collected and returned library books, dismantled stereo equipment, rode off to return a friend's bike, made a series of calls, embraced the relatives he'd lived with, and finally, took me along to meet a friend of his from high school and her young *husband* for a goodbye lunch. At age nineteen and twenty-three respectively, they were expecting a baby in a month and were both enthusiastic and scared about the unplanned path their lives were about to take. As Hudson hugged his friend goodbye, her belly pressed against him, he seemed to slip deeper into melancholy, and he was quiet as we raced for the ferry we were sure to miss.

We finally boarded the ferry two hours after reaching the terminal and, consciously or unconsciously, were apart for most of the voyage, reading and watching the waves on opposite ends of the ship. That night, we stayed in Vancouver with Zoë and her boyfriend in a house full of boxes and spilled belongings. They were packing up and switching residences as they were both starting graduate programs in the fall. Zoë had taken a year off after her degree from Emily Carr and was living and doing commissioned art in the home she shared with her guy and a group of Vancouver artists — yes, some were west coast vegans, but most were transplanted Calgarians. Zoë and her boyfriend would both be studying at the University of British Columbia — she would do her Masters in Fine Art and he would be an architecture student. They were thrilled to be embarking on the next stage in their lives, but on that night, they were weary, and conversation was soft and slow in the dim, cluttered house. Hudson and I left Vancouver for Calgary the next morning under a steady spring rain and a dull sky. Driving through the drizzle along the long, straight highway to Hope, listening to my son's choice of music, I wondered if his mood had changed so much that he had given up the idea of enjoying the trip. A song came on that I was fond of, "Bowl of Oranges."

"I like your music more these days," I ventured. "I liked what you were playing yesterday at the ferry terminal, too."

Exasperated and only slightly amused at my musical ignorance, he told me, "That was the same as this, Mom. It's by Bright Eyes. You always say that about Bright Eyes." We gassed up the Durango in Hope and wound our way onto the town's main street. There is always a feeling of shelter in Hope, the town nestled on a small plain in the Fraser Valley beneath a circle of Cascade Mountains. I led Hudson into a coffee shop I'd discovered on one of the trips I took to get Zoë settled, when I'd been determined to treat myself to better than gas station fare. Hudson ordered yogurt, spinach salad, and water, while I justified my choice of a brownie and cappuccino as necessary for being alert on the road. My children often eat better than me now, a revelation I guiltily try to ignore.

Luxuriating in the heady scent of fresh roasted beans, I chose a table in the front of the coffee shop beside a window looking out to the town's wide street. Hudson's phone chirped a few times as school friends text messaged with that day's plans, forgetting that he was headed east again. Hudson bent his head to deliver speedy responses. I chewed on my brownie, watching a yellow dog run away from its owner in the park across the street. "Hey Mr. Texter, you're popular today," I said, feeling left out of his world.

"Yeah, some people text too much," he said as he turned off the sound on his phone. I was with him on that. It seemed like every coffee shop I entered was full of people looking down at their cells, no one offering a nod or a friendly hello. But despite my reservations about the antisocial elements of texting, I couldn't help but extol it to other moms. A guy could get a text from his mom and acknowledge it with a quick response, and the guys he was hanging with didn't have to know he was checking in.

"Here's some trivia for you, Mom," Hudson said as we walked back to the car. "The first text said, Merry Christmas. But the dudes who invented texting thought it would just enhance pagers. No one thought it would take off the way it has."

"Lily just told me her friend, Samantha, had a boyfriend she was dating for four months who broke up with her via a text."

"Sounds like a loser. She's better off without him."

"I guess. We should get back on the road."

"Do you want me to drive?"

"Maybe later," I said. I drove the car down Main Street and circled back toward the highway. Hudson glanced at his phone again, before leaning back into his seat.

My first feeble attempts at texting occurred sometime after Hudson started university. It was a clumsy start. Early on, Hudson — who turns his spell check off because it's annoying and he doesn't need it — sent me this mocking text, *Mom, lernt to text and spel.* This was before my love affair with the iPhone (thank you, Steve Jobs). At the time, the keyboard on my phone was tiny, three letters to a key, and my thumbs inexperienced. Plus I had autocorrect and my messages were constantly being autocorrected *incorrectly.* Like many a mom, I was also slow to pick up text lingo. I thought I was catching on when I ended a message to Lily with *Peace.* She texted back, *Mom, Peace is like*

Peace Out, when the conversation is over. It does not mean it's the other person's turn to talk. Right.

When Cole was hanging with his snowboarding crew at Whistler or back when Hudson was meeting new students in Victoria, I imagined they heard the ding of my text and knew they could respond swiftly and get back to their lives. I found the success rate was better than that of leaving voicemails. A fact that made sense when Hudson recently shared a secret of youth culture, "Don't leave *voicemails*, Mom. Nobody does that anymore. If I see you've called, I'll call back. But if you leave a voicemail, then I know what you want and I'm less curious."

I was always more likely to get the girls on the phone, but even they prefer texting now because of the unobtrusive way it fits into their busy schedules. Lily flies about her day, phone in hand, writing herself notes, taking photos, updating her calendar, and sending me various friendly, staccato missives or queries. I've seen her pause, an unconscious smile sliding across her face as she reads a flurry of flirty texts from a new guy. Rather than thinking that the guy should telephone my enraptured daughter, I try to view his messages as some form of old-fashioned love letter. Zoë's more likely to not even know where her phone is, but when she locates it, she'll text me asking for help solving a problem or sharing something funny in her day.

On days when I have been busy with my own work, or trying to avoid it, I've sent all my family text missives, having learned through experience to only ever ask one question at a time to increase the odds of receiving an answer. Then I've waited impatiently for the little ding indicating one of them has replied. Sometimes I don't have to bug them. Over the years I have received practical text queries like, "How much milk do you use to scramble two eggs?" I've gotten an ugly photo with an accompanying message, "Does this raw beef look edible or like it's gone bad?" Many times, late at night, my phone will ding with the message, "Mom, you awake?" And I get comfortable in the dark living room for the long phone conversation that will follow.

142

We slowed to a stop as we hit construction on the road ahead. Hudson offered me a piece of gum and checked his phone one more time. As we were waved on, I heard the chirp indicating I had a text message and asked Hudson to read it for me. It was Lily asking for an ETA on when we would reach our cottage in the BC Interior. She and her dad had already arrived and were waiting for us to join them for a weekend at the lake as an interlude during our journey home. "Text them not to wait dinner on us," I directed Hudson. "We're still hours away."

It was shortly after that when I took the wrong highway. I realized it quickly and we could have gone back and made better time by returning to our original route, the new four-lane highway leading to the Coquihalla Pass over the mountains. But the sun was shining and the roads were clear, and I decided to stay on the long, winding, narrow highway that curls through the towns of Spuzzum, Boston Bar, and Spences Bridge at an easier pace. Hudson wasn't aware of my mistake, and when I told him what I'd accidentally done, he didn't react except to ask if I wanted to listen to a Bob Dylan documentary on the car's DVD player. Sure, I said as we drove higher up into a layer of wispy clouds. Hudson had discovered Bob Dylan in his first semester of university, living away from home, and enduring a dark and rainy west coast winter.

I had discovered Dylan in my youth, as well. According to my husband and children, I'm something of an anomaly when it comes to musical appreciation. They have a theory that music doesn't mean very much to me. And I suppose that, except for a crush on Cat Stevens, a passing interest in Barry Manilow, and the influence of a melancholy girlfriend whose life beat to the melodies of Elton John, music is more background for me than it is for them. But I knew the words to Dylan's songs from way back. And Hudson, via phone conversations from his aunt and uncle's place in Victoria, had turned Lily, home from Italy and in grade twelve, onto Dylan at the same time he made his discovery. She had been downloading and searching out all his works so that our house was often filled with the soothing timbre of Dylan's voice. Lily had set her CD alarm clock to wake her to "Hurricane." After school, she would play "House of the Risin' Sun," "It Ain't Me Babe," and "Like A Rolling Stone," and when she fell asleep at night, I'd have to creep into her room to turn his crooning off.

A dappled sunlight broke through the thin clouds as the car crested the mountain top. I saw a small sign beside the road that said Jackass Mountain Summit. I was going to point out the funny name, but Hudson was singing along with Dylan. My kids don't mind telling me that I can't carry a tune, but this time, there was no comment when I joined him on "It's All Over Now, Baby Blue." The commentary continued with reviewers talking about how Dylan resisted being pigeonholed; he didn't like his songs to be considered protest songs. As we sped down the road, I noticed how, even that high up in the mountains, the trees were in fresh spring bud.

"Hey, Hud, isn't it something," I said, thinking back to the night before when Zoë had talked of applying for a teaching position while she did her Masters, "to think about Zoë actually being the teacher to a bunch of first year university students? Can you imagine walking in and having someone as young as Zoë for your teacher?"

"Yeah, I can. I've always thought of Zoë as old. She's my big sister."

It wasn't the response I'd anticipated. I'd hoped to lead into a discussion about teaching being an option for Hudson. He saw through me and blocked my thinly veiled suggestions as if he was still playing defense on his high school football team. "Look, Mom, I can't think about going back to school. I know I'm not doing it this September. I know that for sure." I shut my mouth, certain I'd ruined whatever relaxed mood the music had created.

We stopped to stretch and buy chips, water, and a pack of gum at a gas station in Spence's Bridge. The tiny garage was ripe with the sharp smell of gas and air fresheners. The attendants behind the counter, whose rollicking conversation we'd clearly interrupted, were an old man and a teenage girl. As we were leaving the shabby building, Hudson nudged me, "Wow — synchronicity, eh? Listen." Somewhere under the desk, they had a radio playing Bob Dylan's "A Hard Rain's A-Gonna Fall." We stepped outside with an easiness between us again, talking about feeling goosebumps and what Dylan might think of the coincidence. Leaving town, a sign warned, *Wind Gusts Next 7 km*, but the trees alongside the road barely swayed. All was calm. My favourite Dylan song was being performed on the DVD, or maybe it was just the one most embedded in my memory. I sung out loud, mumbling over any forgotten words. The road ahead of us looked like it was heading off the globe, the pavement meeting the horizon, and it seemed like the car could lift off and glide into the blue sky. "Doesn't it look like we could launch? Like we could just leave the road and fly off over the trees?" I asked over Dylan's voice crooning "Mr. Tambourine Man."

I worried when Hudson didn't respond right away, uncertain whether he was considering the surrounding steel, gray cliffs, and deep valley, or the wide river way below us, but he raised an eyebrow at my psychedelic suggestion and said, "Maybe Dylan was right. Everybody's got to get stoned." He grinned. I had to be patient. My clever son would find his path.

Chapter 15

Teenage Runaway

You and dad are really the wrecking ball of all of our outlaw, runaway fantasies. Why couldn't you jerks go and be crack addicts or religious fanatics so we could have excuses to live on the wide open road?

– Email from Lily

This is a story of all the ways and times my kids left home, but there is a chapter I thought best to leave out until Lily granted me her permission to put it in. "It's okay, Mom," she said. "It will add drama. I'm happy to supply some drama. Just as long as you remember in the telling of it, that was then. This is now."

This is the story of Lily running away — only she, of course, never calls it that. Much to her chagrin, the rest of the family does. I try not to think about it too often, the way you do with times in your life when you are so terribly off balance. In fact, those sixty odd, uneasy days when Lily ran away were the first time we had a completely empty nest.

For twenty-three years, one month and twenty-nine days, I was a mom with children living at home. In the early autumn of her seventeenth year, Lily was going to be the last kid still residing with her dad and me. After a summer of living with us and doing lucrative summer jobs in Calgary, both Cole and Hudson had returned to the coast. Hudson had moved in with a bunch of guys in Victoria, and Cole, elated to be starting a film production program in Vancouver, was renting a room in the house Zoë and her boyfriend lived in. As I look back on it all, there had been some foreshadowing of Lily's departure before she left home in the middle of the night without saying goodbye.

To be fair, Lily would tell it differently. She woke me up at two a.m., putting her face up close to mine to whisper that she couldn't find her social security card and needed it for a new job she was applying for early the next morning. She went on to explain to me in my groggy haze that she was going to stay over at a girlfriend's near the job's location. I stumbled out of bed, despite her telling me not to. Standing in the light of the hallway, Lily told me she loved me and gave me a long hug, apologizing for disturbing my sleep. You are not a mother for twenty-three years, one month and twenty-nine days (Zoë's age) without knowing something is bloody well up when that sequence of events takes place, but somehow I fell back into bed and had the last restful sleep I would have for weeks.

The next afternoon was glorious and sunny, and I was sitting with a close friend eating spanakopitas and calamari at our favourite Greek place, assuming Lily was working at the photo store, when Cole called from Vancouver. And, yes, unlike my chatty daughters, the boys don't often phone midday without a purpose or query so I excused myself and picked up, but Cole seemed only to want to know how I was and what I was doing with my September afternoon. A few minutes later, Hudson called with the same hesitant "what's up with your day" sort of inquiry. "This is crazy," I told my good friend. Just as we were ready to order our baklava, my phone chirped indicating that I had a text from Lily. "Mom," she had written, "I told some friends I could drive them to Vancouver. We're going to stay at the cottage tonight. Back in a couple of days. Don't worry." I almost choked on my squid. My friend, the mother of two teenage daughters, was as alarmed as I was, and motioned for me to pick up quickly when Zoë called as well. Our motherly "spidey senses" were going berserk. I was so bent on sending Lily the sternest text my fingers could tap out that I didn't even know if I could pause to speak with Zoë. "Hey, Mom…" Zoë began, attempting the same phony, calm voice her brothers had employed, but she had a better female understanding of both her sister and me and her "how's your day going?" was strained.

"Look, I've heard from Lily now," I said.

"Oh, and so you know…"

"I know she's halfway to Vancouver and has friends with her and…"

"So you do know," Zoë interrupted, then proceeded to provide a deluge of confusing information. "Look, Lily told Cole and Hudson her ridiculous plan. Hudson promised her he wouldn't tell you, but he told me. He wanted me to figure out what you knew, so that it wouldn't really be him telling on Lily." Zoë was breathless, rushing to get it all off her big-sister chest. "I wanted to tell you last week that Lily called me asking if she could freakin' live in the jeep, but park it at our house and use our shower, cause she said you said she couldn't just show up here and not pay rent, and that you wanted her to save money from home before moving out anywhere." Zoë was as nervous as I was. Since both Cole and Hudson graduated at seventeen-and-a half, Will and I had learned a thing or two about such young high school grads and their commitment to university. With Lily the same age and finished high school, we had strongly discouraged her from even considering beginning any of the university programs she'd been talking about. Take a break from school, earn some money, travel, be free for a while, we had merrily suggested. (Here's where I stick in that piece of advice again: don't let your kids start grade school too young lest they finish high school too early.) Lily's grand escape wasn't a complete surprise. Several times over the summer, she had asked me whether it would be okay for her to move to Vancouver, and I'd told her each and every time that after she worked at home to raise the first and last month's rent required to move into her own place, she could do as she pleased. She wasn't an adult yet, but she had finished high school. When she asked if she could land at the house her brother, sister, and sister's boyfriend shared with three other roommates, I had told her, "No. Bad idea." All those others paid rent, and she couldn't be the freeloader on the couch. In retrospect — and I had a lot of long, sleepless nights to think back — I honestly believe this was only fair to the others in the house, but hey, I won't deny I wanted her to stay home for a while longer and not have all my kids gone so soon.

So, of course, I knew what this youngest daughter of mine was up to. My stomach was churning as I feigned interest in the baklava. My friend, who'd known our exuberant and dramatic Lily since she was born, encouraged me to get busy texting and was on the edge of her seat assisting my long distance parenting. In my text, I made sure there was no doubt that I was mad that Lily hadn't made her father and me aware of her plans before executing them, and that, though she was the only kid at home and therefore the only one that used the little jeep (a stick shift I didn't drive), she absolutely should have asked permission to take it so far away. I was able to weakly laugh as Lily's brothers called again with unrelated queries. Keeping up the pretense that no one was squealing, I filled them in on their sister's sudden departure, and they responded with appropriate worry.

That evening, Will called Lily at the cottage where she was holed up with her friends — more than halfway along the twelve hour route to Vancouver. He furiously played the heavy, insisting Lily bring the car back immediately. Of course, what we both wanted, finding ourselves alone months before we planned, was for Lily to come back — it was hardly about the stupid car. But we were forced to make that our case, because as young as she was and as not ready for her departure as we were, Lily was fully graduated from high school, had been employed for two and a half months, and had earned enough money to fund her own exploits.

Just short of straight-up defiance, Lily insisted that she just had to get her travelling companions to Vancouver as promised, and she would get the jeep back to us if we really were set against her using it; however, she was, in fact, moving to Vancouver. Acting as if it was the missing car that was most infuriating him, Will told Lily how disappointed he was in her, directing her to hand it over to her brother, Cole, immediately upon her arrival in Vancouver, and hoped, without wheels, she would tire of her adventure more expediently.

There being no doubt how irate her dad was with her, Lily did as she'd been told and let Cole take procession of our red jeep (lucky him). During those first turbulent days, Will and I both had trouble concentrating on anything. He called me more frequently from work but not to say much of anything, just to ask if I'd heard anything new from Lily or her siblings.

I found myself either sitting still for long periods of time or the opposite, throwing myself into a momentous task. I started clearing out the garden and re-organizing the garage, but I choked partway through, leaving a mound of uprooted perennials and gone-to-seed vegetables amongst the autumn flowers, and a stack of kid's tattered sporting equipment and broken skateboards piled high in the garage as an irritating reminder of my distracted state.

We learned from Cole that Lily had hooked up with friends she had made visiting Zoë in Vancouver the summer before. She had somehow found, to our huge surprise and frustrated disappointment, a "room" to rent that was incredibly cheap. Two hundred dollars a month cheap, a price that had her siblings worried. "You don't ever find rent like that in this city," Zoë informed me, "unless it's a real hole."

Lily and I weren't exactly communicating very well just then. Well, I was communicating, and Lily was only sometimes responding. That said, my texts looked something like this, "Lily, your dad and I have almost stopped sleeping at night. This is the oddest thing you have ever done. We're worried about your health and safety. Please call."

Her texts, much less frequent than mine, looked more like this, "It's not that odd, Mom. Chill out." Cole and Lily shared the same extroverted nature and desire for ever expanding social circles, and so they usually connected and chilled well together.

"Mom, you've got to harass her less, I'm thinking," he admonished me on the phone. "She says you're sending her a zillion mean texts. Lily just needs to shake things up a bit. You know, don't you remember what I was like a while back?" But thinking about Cole's days of travelling didn't help. As I was attempting to breathe in through my nose and out through my mouth, he added, "Though we have to get her to move. You don't even want to see the skanky area she's in. It's totally sketchy. In fact," he said, protectively of me, "don't ever go there. I'll deal with it."

Will has a strong protective streak where his daughters are concerned and so sometimes I soften the truth of their exploits, but he called me as I was distractedly grocery shopping and, in a moment of weakness, leaning against a huge crate of pumpkins, I let loose with what I'd heard from both Cole and Zoë about Lily's choice of residence. I immediately felt horrible for sharing my feeling of dread. "She did live in Rome without us," I offered weakly.

"Yeah, with a host family. And a pseudo mom and dad, and a home in a good neighbourhood, and she was communicating with us on a regular basis. It was nothing like this."

Staring down the barrel of his youngest daughter's mutiny and more worried every day, Will drummed up a countermove — he sent me to chase her down, suggesting I take the next flight. I elected to drive, hoping the journey through the mountains amid the changing fall colours would let me arrive at Zoë's house feeling more Zen. It's possible that I was calmer and more contemplative when I arrived, willing to open my mind to the idea that Lily was stretching her proverbial wings, until Zoë's boyfriend, a tall, fit twenty-five-year-old, told me he wouldn't walk around where Lily was living in broad daylight.

Lily texted me back in a nanosecond when I offered to take her for lunch and, to my utter surprise, asked me if I wanted to pick her up at her "house" so she could show it to me. She gave me an address in the notorious East Hastings area — but the downtown part of Hastings, she said. "You can see people dressed up in business suits just a block or so away." This was true. Sloping up the street from the address Lily gave me, if I cranked my neck to look past the infamous "Needle Park," I could view where the shitty and awful part of Hastings transformed into the business area of downtown Vancouver. Lily's building was the beginning of the shitty, awful part. My youngest daughter used to get a kick out of touring show homes. When she was a little kid, I'd pick her up after her choir practice, and we'd walk through the nearby show suites, playing a game she made up where we were supposed to imagine that she and I were shopping for a new condo just for us. (It is a fantasy particular to big families — one that any of us might have indulged in when life was too noisy and chaotic.) The idea that Lily was now eager to tour me through her apartment in one of the most impoverished, drug-addled — sketchiest — areas in all of Vancouver seemed like some kind of sick twist on her childhood game.

A few weeks earlier, I had visited Hudson in Victoria where he had taken up residence in a large rundown home, which the landlord had admitted was slated for demolition but was oddly situated in an upscale newer suburb that included stylish seniors' lodges. The contrast to Lily's new living situation was extreme. True, her building was located just one short block from where West Hastings met East Hastings, but the neighbourhood was clearly a haven for the homeless and, as far as I could tell, some sort of sanctuary for what my kid's generation referred to as crackheads. "The homeless are really harmless," Lily told me later, but the first time I drove down the block of East Hastings that she lived on, I was shocked. Not just shocked as in I was registering surprise, but shocked like my breathing sped up, my heart raced, and I started perspiring. A whole village of impoverished people appeared to be camped on the street corners in the middle of the day. As I pulled to the curb, a teenage girl sat down on the sidewalk beside my car, as if to catch her breath, and asked if I had any spare change. I gave her a few bucks and told her to buy a sandwich. A deathly pale woman in a dirty pink hoodie was searching for something on the road, wandering back and forth over the same four feet. Another elderly woman, wrapped in a layer of blankets, wandered into the street, oblivious to traffic. There were lots of men, too, but I was focused on the women. I texted Lily that I was there, standing near the metal screen that protected the red door behind which, she said, were the stairs up to her place. When she didn't text back, I phoned her. No answer. I was frantic. She was safe when we spoke two hours ago, but anything could have happened. I debated calling Cole, not to have him worry, but because he had more contact with her than I did. Then the red door was opening, and I saw Lily's arms reaching round to undo the lock on the heavy chain holding the metal screen closed. She was waving and grinning. She bent down to nudge a person sleeping in the doorway aside and shrugged up at me. That was when I saw that her eyes were red and runny. She hugged me hard, and I wrapped my arms around her perhaps thinner than usual frame. I listened to her sniffle as I followed her back up the long set of stairs.

"So, what do you think?" It wasn't a home or apartment but a vacuous dim space scattered with empty bottles. Three or four bikes leaned against a wall, along with a wheelchair; desks and mismatched shelves lined another wall. Plastic lawn chairs sat here and there, and the pièce de résistance was two long skateboard ramps arcing across the middle of the room. "Lily, who lives here?"

"Different people. Mostly artists. One guy's away tree planting."

"So it's some sort of drop-in place?"

Lily rolled her eyes. "People pay rent, Mom. The landlord has an art gallery downstairs. Sometimes the artists stay here." Far off to one side were three rooms. Lily led me to the third. "This is my room," she said. "I'd get some art and find a dresser or whatever, but I don't spend that much time in here." Of course, she didn't. There was only one window, and it faced not outside but back into the larger space, and the bed was makeshift and covered with a pile of blankets. Lily, who is fanatically clean and a worshipper of sunlight, was residing here? It got stranger. "Look, Mom," she said, reaching down and grabbing a long-haired white cat that circled her ankles, "his name is Whatever."

"But, Lily," I protested, "you hate cats. You don't ever touch cats. You're so allergic to cats."

"Whatever," my daughter said, sniffling more and blinking tears from her irritated eyes. "So, do you think this place is cool?"

Was this one of those times when I should have counted to ten or twenty, or a thousand, before answering? Maybe, but I didn't. "No, it's not cool, Lily, and I can't imagine that it's legal. It's dark and weird. Don't you think it's dark and weird?" I asked, crushing any chance of having a nice visit.

"I was going to ask if you wanted to see the bathroom, but forget it."

"No, show me the bathroom."

"Forget it." She pulled her hair into a ponytail and grabbed her hoodie. "I thought you were a cool mom who would appreciate my first place. But you're being like a typical mom. And mean."

That's what I was — mean and not cool. She picked up her big bag, and I followed her down the dark stairway — only Lily skipped down ahead of me and pulled the metal screen shut between us. "If you're not nice, I could lock you in here," she laughed.

"I'd just go hang out in your place, maybe ride the bike on the skateboard ramp."

"Funny, Mom. But you can't. It's locked at the top. You'd be stuck in the stairway." The whole family knows I am claustrophobic. Lily saw that I wasn't terribly amused and pushed the metal door open, releasing me into the street. We drove to a restaurant that I knew Lily liked. She asked if she could order a steak and mashed potatoes, and, of course, I said yes. This was when I finally did my counting, trying to figure out how to get Lily to explain her poor choices and to let me know her future intentions. Despite my slow and careful approach, I found the conversation quickly going off the rails when I stupidly used the cat as evidence that Lily had lost her mind.

"It's just bizarre behavior, Lily. Cats make you so miserable that you say you hate them. Now you're hugging them?"

"Whatever," she said, smiling.

"Though I guess I'm relieved. When I saw you all sniffling and your eyes running and living where you live, I thought maybe you were doing meth or something horrible."

"Oh my God, Mom, I didn't go from attending high school so recently, doing all my homework, mostly never getting into trouble, and telling you everything, to doing meth."

"Okay, you just live on the same street as people who do that."

"Yeah, I guess. But there really is an art gallery downstairs."

"Why do you ignore most of my texts?"

"Because you're bugging me. All those texts about how I should text and call, and asking whether I'm eating and talking to Zoë and Cole. Can't you just ask me how my day is going? Or what the weather is like?"

"Lily, you're freaking us out. I can't sleep at night. Dad looks like a wreck."

"I have to grow up sometime."

I wanted to scream. How do you make a seventeen-year-old get it? How do you define what it is?

There were two people lying in front of Lily's doorway when I dropped her off. As freaked out as I was, I admired how gently she nudged them aside to get at the lock. I dreaded telling Will the details of our daughter's new residence. His paternal instincts were already in extreme overdrive. Some of his peers at work who he'd confided in told him he should just go out there and drag her butt back home. All of them had grade school kids, kids they watched play soccer games and accompanied to birthday parties on Saturdays, kids too young for mysterious teenage lives and almost adult aspirations, kids who hadn't challenged their need to protect them yet. That night, I confessed Lily's new address to our Vancouver friends who had put Zoë up when she first arrived as a student. "You don't want her there," they said. "Get her out of there." Will had already decided to fly in for the weekend. Normally, I don't mind being the chief negotiator with the kids, but I was more than ready to take on a co-pilot for Operation: Make Lily Move.

During Lily's home/warehouse tour, she had neglected to mention that the joint only had cold running water. She showed up to shower at Zoë's just before her dad arrived. Freshly scrubbed and shampooed, Lily bounced into her dad's arms and he offered to take her for lunch, while the rest of us hung back, aware that the interrogation was about to begin.

Will later recounted what happened next as something like this. He really was taking her for lunch to try to talk sense into her and, if that didn't work, to absolutely insist that she move to a safer area. He was going to explain how unfair it was to worry us all and how he thought that she was naive enough to still need some parental guidance. But, he told me, she was lulled to sleep in the car by stop-and-go traffic, and he got worried that he wouldn't succeed in convincing her to listen. As he gazed at her sleeping, he thought she was still just a kid, maybe starting down the wrong path, maybe not. He couldn't let her spend one more night in the place I'd described, and, thinking about his friend's advice, suddenly he was on a rescue mission. He started heading out of the city with Lily and my car, planning — as much as he was planning anything — to somehow make Lily come to her senses when she woke up, maybe around Hope, and they'd have a nice drive home through the mountains. (I would have to fly back.) But Lily woke up and went crazy, sobbing, yelling, and accusing him of tricking her. She couldn't see that in his overprotective way, he was attempting to save her. He pulled over nowhere near Hope and asked her to promise to move her things over to Zoë's house and stay there until she found a better place in a safe, or at least safer, neighbourhood.

Meanwhile, Cole and I had walked through the fall leaves to a neighbourhood pub, and, over potato skins and drinks, he told me all about his cinematography classes and we discussed our favourite movies, pretending that Quentin Tarantino was more on our minds than Lily and Will. Returning, we approached Zoë's deck to find the roommates sitting there; they raised their eyebrows and nodded toward the living room, as if there was something to be wary of inside.

Lily was leaning against her dad on the couch. The roommates had heard the whispered story of the botched rescue from Zoë, who Lily had texted on the way back into the city. They must have found Will and Lily sitting together like that, propping each other up, odd. But I believe Lily had just rediscovered the depth of her dad's crushing love for her and had battled with the friction between that and her need for independence, leading to some sort of wild truce being formed that had left them both equally spent but hanging on to each other there in the corner of the big couch in Zoë's living room.

We ordered Thai food for everyone and ate it quietly, before Will instructed Cole to assist Lily in getting her things out of her warehouse room on Hastings the following day. I took Will back to the airport that night and promised I'd join him in our empty nest soon. There wasn't a spare room or bed in the house that Zoë, her boyfriend, Cole, and three other roommates now shared with Lily. I assumed Lily would sleep on the couch when the house was finally quiet that night, but she later told me, no, the couch wasn't that comfortable and her brother let her sleep beside him in his basement bedroom.

I gave Zoë, Cole, and Hudson the opportunity to divulge their youthful thoughts on their first forays away from home. Zoë shared her sentiments with listeners of the CBC, Cole surprised me with his revelations of feeling so young on the slopes of Whistler, and Hudson made my heart hurt with his tale of leaving behind the girl he'd pined for since seventh grade. It was only fair to give Lily the opportunity to share what was on her mind when she "ran away," but I almost didn't ask her, reasoning that she had shared her high school immersion experience through emails from Rome. Still, she had her host mom then, and she was just sixteen and there were rules. So I held my breath and asked Lily if she would like to add her perspective on "running away" to Vancouver. I made those quote signs with my fingers, and she cringed and laughed. Her side of the story went like this:

So when I was seventeen and had just finished high school, I begged my parents to let me do a week-long trip to visit my friend, Mattie, in Vancouver. I bought the ticket with money I'd earned working as a photo lab technician — which is a good job for an aspiring photographer just out of high school. I went on the trip and had so much fun, although I don't remember the details of it specifically other than it was the first time I had ever tried quail. Mattie's dad was a very classy guy who had recently become a quadriplegic and had a nurse/girlfriend who helped him cut up and eat his quail. I remember thinking that this bird was way too big of a pain in the ass to eat. Too little yield for all that work. (I feel the same way about pomegranates and chicken wings.)

I returned to Calgary and about a week later was at a bar frequented by high school-aged minors (also unironically a favourite of pedophiles and ravenous creepy dudes). I was talking to two skater guys (also underaged) who I was loosely acquainted with, and they were saying that they were going to hitchhike to Vancouver the next day. I launched into how much I loved Vancouver and how badly I wanted to go back, and suddenly suggested the brilliant plan that I would drive these two not-quite strangers to their destination — we would all seek our manifest destinies together. Knowing that my parents would never in a million years allow me to move to Vancouver with zero notice, zero plan, and almost zero dollars, I raced home to throw everything I felt I couldn't live without into the family jeep I shared with my brothers when they were home. I woke up my mom — maybe slightly on purpose — and gave her a guilty hug in the hallway before escaping into the night to meet my fellow travellers at the proposed meeting spot. We set out and I soon realized that neither of the boys could drive stick worth shit (I stopped to test their skills in a McDonald's parking lot — they failed), so I would be behind the wheel. The guys DJed straight classic rock the whole way, and one of them sang every song at the top of his lungs — it was actually really sweet, even though I thought he was insane (I wasn't wrong). We made an overnight stop at our family cabin and grabbed a bottle of wine from the cellar to open upon our arrival in Vancouver and drink in celebration.

When we got to Vancouver, our first stop was the skate park downtown — the Plaza, it's called. One of the guys opened the back of the jeep to grab the boards, and the wine tumbled out and smashed on the pavement in a big purple splat. My mom is big on good luck omens, but I think we need to be aware of bad luck ones, too. This omen was not beyond me. I knew that my adventure in Vancouver was coming at the cost of my parents' trust in me, but my frontal lobe-deficient brain considered it a small price to pay for what I felt in my heart was the right thing for me at the time.

I still hold that moving to Vancouver was the right thing for me; I just realize now that I went about it completely wrong. I'm probably a textbook Capricorn youngest child and stubbornly hate being accused of having a stubborn streak.

As night fell, the guys got over skateboarding, and we heard of a party that was happening in some artist warehouse. I drove the jeep, still full of my belongings, and parked it in a really sketchy downtown parking lot close to the party, which was on Hastings. East Hastings in Vancouver is possibly the most horrific display of a congregation of crackheads in North America. But the neighbourhoods where there are the most crackheads are also the neighbourhoods where young people can afford to live. The party was fun. Many of the guests were on acid and being very nice. I walked with a cute skater guy about five years my senior to his place, where he couldn't find his key, so we slept in his backyard until daybreak, at which point his roommate let him in and he promptly fell asleep on the couch. I liked him, and in an act of teenage desperation to see him again, I wrote my number out in matchsticks (couldn't find a pen) on the coffee table. He never called. Probably a good thing.

A few days later, I wound up back at the warehouse where the party had been. It was this rundown building; the main floor was occupied by a very nice artsy hippy guy named Chester, and the loft upstairs was rented out by various skaters and artists. Now, I see it for what it was — a squat house for artistic idealists with no money. To a seventeen-year-old, this place was a dream. It was right downtown, walking distance to all the bars and parties. There were mini-ramps, collections of antiques, and a plethora of bikes that had been bought for five dollars a piece from crackheads (my favourite was this little blue low-rider bike with white wheels — probably originally owned by some seven-year-old kid — which I used to ride around the loft in circles). The building had this big, red cast iron gate on the street level that had to be wrapped diligently with padlocks and chains when you left to keep the crackheads from breaking (more of) the windows. I came to live at "The Red Gate" because I got along incredibly well with one of the tenants there, a guy named Eddie.

Eddie was a painter; he also skated and loved rap and weed. I was reading Helter Skelter at the time, and my immediate love of Eddie reminded me of Manson — the power he had, how people wanted to be around him. Eddie was like that but without the whole sadistic murderer thing going on. Eddie would never hurt a fly. I still think he's one of the sweetest, most understanding, and welcoming people I've ever met. I felt totally at ease with him. He would tell me I'm beautiful and give me all sorts of compliments, and I never once felt like he was hitting on me or wanted anything from me at all. I immediately trusted him. He told me that one of the girls who used to live there had disappeared without a word to anyone, and so her room was unoccupied. I helped Chester out with scanning some artwork, and he paid me for that, which I turned around and gave back as cheap rent. There was no kitchen and no hot water. Although there was a room with a shower, it had no light. Once or twice, I brought a candle in there and tried showering in freezing cold water, but that gave me a headache. Chester usually just let us shower downstairs in his bathroom where the water was hot. Of course, I would never put up with all this shit now. I have a better sense of how much it costs to live in a clean apartment with hot water and a working stove, with no crackheads fighting below your window and no rats and stray cats scuttling around in dark corners.

Fact is, I would never, ever want to live in that part of Vancouver again. I'm allergic to cats and it seemed like everyone had one or two. I hate rain even more than snow, and it rains in Vancouver for weeks on end, and almost everyone in the crowd I hung with had dreads and really shitty piercings — which have always skeeved me out. The thought of metal going through flesh makes me squeamish. Theft is a huge problem on the Lower Eastside because of all of the crack. You see young kids doing blow and molly in dark corners from Wednesday to Saturday. However, I digress.

Back then, I had about two hundred dollars to my name and an irrepressible urge to have fun. I was so thrilled to be through with high school. When I did my exchange in Rome in grade eleven, I barely had to do any school work; my biggest academic task was to learn Italian. I managed that and went to contemporary photography exhibits. I walked around Rome by myself, freshly sixteen, ordering cuba libres at bars and tasting free wine, before watching the sunset above St. Peter's Basilica every night. Then I would return to my host home for an episode of The Simpsons dubbed in Italian, a world-class dinner, and bed. I fell asleep at night with my windows wide open, listening to the sounds of motorinos and classy, boisterous women in heels on cobblestones. So going back to regular school after that was draining my life force — I had tasted freedom. When I went to Vancouver on my own after graduation, I felt it come rushing back, and no number of crackheads or cats was going to keep me from MY NEW LIFE. I got a job at a popular clothing store where I was annoyed by my M.I.A (a female British recording artist) obsessed coworkers, but we got free tickets to shows at the Commodore. I took photos constantly and had a couple of photo shows myself at "The Red Gate"; everyone was always so eager to meet the new girl.

When I couldn't shower at Chester's, I would make my way across town to Zoë's house and freeload courtesy of her domestic security. Cole was living there, too. I guess he was assigned to keep tabs on me, which was okay. I didn't mind answering Cole's texts. Mom's were getting annoying. About a month in, I was curled up with Eddie in a patch of sunlight streaming in from the high windows, just chatting and ignoring the madness on the street below, when I got a panicked call from Cole to say that Mom was in town and he didn't think I should let her see where I lived. Part of all the craziness was that I decided to share it with her, to invite her up. Next thing I knew, Dad was flying in to rescue me, and I was leaving "The Red Gate" and sleeping in the basement of Zoë's house with my brother. That sounds strange in most people's worlds, but I've always considered it a moving testament to my brother's love for me that when everyone was worried, he shared his sleeping space without complaint.

Months later, I was sitting on the couch at my parent's house during the holidays talking to one of my dad's best friends. He was laying a heavy guilt trip on me, saying that I had put a lot of gray hairs on my dad's head when I took off to Vancouver. I'll never forget that conversation and how badly I felt, recognizing the unquestionable truth in those words. But there I was, nodding my head and already planning to get out of town again — though more gently this time.

So Lily achieved her original goal of joining two of her three siblings in the house where they lived in Vancouver. I don't believe anyone pushed her to look for another place after that. She was encouraged to contribute something toward rent — whatever you pay to curl up small in your brother's bed so that he might not notice that you're there — and to pitch in for groceries (or eat the bruised fruit and vegetables the dumpster-diving roommate brought home).

Midway through November, Lily called from a coffee shop she was holed up in during a downpour on her walk "home" from her retail job. She'd caught me at home, spaghetti sauce simmering on the stove, transfixed by the newscast on the little kitchen TV. A small Canadian cruise ship, whose mission was to retrace the route of the explorer Shackleton, had hit an iceberg in Antarctica the previous night. All of the passengers had been rescued from the sinking ship. The video coverage was poor, but I could make out the ship's red hull listing heavily against the gray water and a long line of bright orange lifeboats bobbing on the calm but frigid ocean, waiting to be rescued by two large cruise ships travelling toward them.

I muted the TV to pay attention to Lily. It had been two and a half months since she had run away, though she never wanted us to refer to it that way. We had gotten back to texting each other often — calm texts about how we were doing, the weather, and friends we were hanging with. When I wanted to know if she looked okay or was eating, or whether her allergies were an issue, I asked Zoë, who long ago had accepted the position of second mother.

"Mom?" Lily said from the coffee shop that wet day.

"Yeah, Lily?"

"All it does here is rain. Cole's got a sorta girlfriend. She doesn't talk to me much."

"Well, you are sharing her boyfriend's bed."

"He's my brother."

"Still."

"I know. I was thinking of coming back, getting a job or even two with sweet tips, and maybe doing a trip to Europe before I have to save for school. You know, backpacking or whatever and staying in hostels. Do you think Dad would be okay with that?"

"I think we could help him be okay with it. You could stay with some of the people you met in Rome and that German exchange student you met here, and you could meet up with your cousin who will be travelling, too."

"I was thinking all that. Maybe Dad would be okay with it if you met up with me as well. Just for a week or so. Maybe in France or something. I've seen some really cheap flights online. Charlotte's mom met her in France. She said it was good."

(I was quietly thrilled to no longer be an intruder in her life.)

"Would you want to?" Lily asked me.

"I'll run it by Dad. Of course, I'd want to."

"I miss my room. I miss knowing where all my stuff is. I'm tired of the rain."

"Well, you did it. You lived in Vancouver."

Lily did do her backpacking trip to Europe and was accepted to university in Montreal. During her second year of school there, I visited her in her small Montreal studio apartment to help her celebrate her twentieth birthday during a bitterly cold January. Coming in from a grocery trip, I stomped the snow from my feet and took a few steps in before I unloaded my bags. Lily was studying on her neatly made bed. "Mom, do you mind wiping your tracks with that cloth beside the hand vacuum?" She used the little appliance to vacuum her four-by-six-foot Ikea rug. Before making us dinner, I started to wash a few dishes in the kitchen sink. "It's okay, Mom," Lily said from the bed, "I'll do the dishes after we eat."

The kitchen was hardly a kitchen at all; it was easier for me to cook with it tidy. "I'll just do them, Lily, before I start."

"Mom, I'm trying not to be fussy," said Lily, whose middle name could have been Fussy, "but I think my method is better for getting grease off the glasses." She left her books to demonstrate. It was then that I asked her if she could explain what she had been doing two years previous in that warehouse room without hot water, sleeping beneath someone else's collection of dusty blankets. "Desperate times, Mom. Desperate times called for desperate measures." She laughed, flicking sudsy water at me. "Everyone was telling me I couldn't do what I wanted to do. I just wanted to be near Cole and Zoë and live in a new city. I didn't want to hurt your feelings and I never meant to freak everyone out." She put the last glass on the rack and looked at me. "Seventeen-year-olds do stupid shit. Sorry," she said with her best apologetic grin, still as thin and allergic to cats as when I worried that she was a starving meth addict.

Chapter 16

A New Chapter

Mom, no one's made a zombie movie from your perspective.
Okay — you're trying to deal with your kids moving out.
There's been an attack on Calgary. It's a B plot. We'll start
with your character going down into the basement where you
have guns. You just have to make it to the cabin and then
repopulate the world. Yeah, it could be a happy ending.

– Cole

It has occurred to me that perhaps this part of the story isn't about one of my kids so much as it is about me. There is a heap of criticism out there of my generation's parenting skills — for our hovering and our helicopter-ing and for bubble wrapping our children. Certainly I have done some of that. But somehow Zoë, Cole, Hudson, and Lily have all managed to zigzag through the helicopter blades and, with loud smacks, pop the bubbles in the wrap in order to seize independence.

I thought about my tendency to hover while trying to sleep on Lily's tiny couch in Montreal, listening to the chaotic street sounds outside of the stifling hot apartment we'd rented for her to live in during her first year of university. Lily had managed to travel to Europe with hardly any interference from us at home. When she returned from Vancouver, she had waitressed, saved her money, celebrated her eighteen birthday, and — with our blessings (well, mine more than her nervous father's) — flew to Barcelona to meet up with friends who had been living in Spain for a couple of months. Her dad and I optimistically pictured her in a Spanish grotto among a group of large Canadians who were seasoned travellers and whose sole purpose was to take care of her. We tried not to think that she might be living with a bunch of scrawny yahoos who may or may not give a rat's ass about her safety. Barcelona is a skateboarding mecca, which was what drew her new Vancouver friends to the city, as well as youth from around the world. Not surprisingly, it also has a reputation in the world of skateboarding photography, right up Lily's alley. Disliking the hostel scene because of the number of rules and (back to her true self) possible germs, Lily successfully rented a friend-of-a-friend's flat with the stipulation that he would move out of it and in with his girlfriend for Lily's two week stay. She ditched her backpack before leaving Barcelona to meet her cousin in Amsterdam, reporting via email that she just couldn't carry that load on her back and had made a deal for a cheap suitcase with wheels in a Spanish marketplace.

Her cousin and his girlfriend's relationship was being tested by the twenty-four/seven-ness of travel, and in order to avoid the volatile tension between them, Lily left Amsterdam shortly after their rendezvous at the Flying Pig Hostel. My sister-in-law was privy to all this drama thanks to her new Facebook page. Lily travelled alone from Holland to Hanover, Germany, where she was being hosted like royalty by the parents of an exchange student she had befriended at high school — big plates of schnitzel, spaetzle, and hot potato salad (if a bit too much sauerkraut), and a bed in one of the cleanest and tidiest homes she had ever been in.

When I had left my parents to travel Europe at the same age, I understood them to be a bit nervous, but in my youthful innocence, I assumed they were also happy, even excited, to see me off on my grand adventure. They later informed me they were scared out of their minds; the smiles pasted on their faces were all the normalcy they could muster. Back then, an adventure required a void of communication. There were no emails to reassure them — I sent brief handwritten letters and postcards along the way, most of which they received after I'd flown home. They rarely heard from me in the ninety days that I was away. When Lily and Cole travelled to faraway places, they used internet cafes to link up with home. While I received obligatory check-ins, I'm sure they typed up tales of wild adventure for their friends. Still those trips, with beginnings and ends, amounted to months, not years. So when Lily returned from her European travels and was accepted into Concordia University in Montreal, three time zones away, I felt it was a new chapter for the two of us. The other three had gone to school in Alberta and British Columbia, but of course, Lily was the last one to ever stick close to home.

I went out to help her search for an apartment in Montreal where she would live for eight school terms (she would sublet and spend the summers at home). Despite, or maybe because of her brief stay in the trashy Vancouver warehouse room, she agreed with my requirement that it feel safe. Lily and I started our search with a walk through the streets of downtown Montreal: Boulevard de Maisonneuve, Rue Guy, Rue Saint Marc, and Avenue du Parc. Using our fledgling grade twelve French, we greeted shopkeepers and landlords with badly accented bonjours, spurring most francophone Montrealers to effortlessly switch to their almost perfect English. Lily would attend an English university in the French core of the city.

Montreal has a fascinating, cross-cultural history. In 1535, the French explorer Jacques Cartier climbed up the small mountain on the fifty-kilometre-long and sixteen-kilometre-wide island in the St. Lawrence River and placed a cross on it, claiming the land in the name of France and naming the mountain Mont-Royal. (Of course, the Iroquois had been there for centuries previous.) The island was subsequently colonized by the French during the early 1600s, and the city of Montreal was founded. Every Canadian kid learns about the British defeating the French colonists in the battle on the Plains of Abraham in Quebec City in 1759, though with a different twist depending on which province they are being taught in. The French weren't expelled but lived in Quebec as subjects of the British Empire, along with settlers from England, Scotland, and Ireland. In 1969, Prime Minister Pierre Elliot Trudeau helped to make Canada fully bilingual and amended the constitution to guarantee Francophone rights.

Discovering the French-ness of Montreal was a treat in an otherwise frustrating and uncomfortably overheated search. Leaving one antiquated top floor apartment just off the popular St. Catherine Street, I was seriously afraid I would die of heat exhaustion if I didn't seek fresh air. With my muddled historical knowledge of Montreal, I knew the buildings would be ancient compared to Calgary's, but I thought that would mean they were charming, rather than material for lucid bad dreams. We first viewed a studio apartment on the edge of being within a reasonable distance from the university. It was also on the edge of a residential street that turned into a concrete freeway, so that Lily would reside almost under an overpass, like Woody Allan's character Alvy Singer, living under the rollercoaster. A jittery old female landlord had us follow her up two long flights of stairs in her deceptively nice on-the-outside character building. One of the only three sentences she mumbled at us was to watch out for the one tall step in the middle of the stairway. (Creepy.) We followed her at a laboriously slow pace down the hallway to the room at the end. She unlocked the apartment door and stepped aside to let us take a look. The space was stale and derelict. She waved toward the interior and, pointing at a hairy old couch, growled, "You can have it if you want." True, Lily had survived her short stint in an East Hastings dive, but I think even that had a certain rebellious cache, with its skateboard ramps and artist tenants, compared to this depressing hovel more suitable to a lonely bachelor uncle with dark secrets.

I mouthed to Lily, "We've got to get out of here," and scampered back down the hall toward the light, with Lily giggling in shock behind me.

We searched Craigslist and the McGill and Concordia university websites more desperately. Behind the regal campus of McGill University, in the centre of Montreal, is an area referred to as the McGill ghetto which, despite the title, is considered acceptable, even coveted, student housing. Lovely cottonwood trees line the narrow streets and what were once grand homes have, over many decades, been converted to student apartments. A few respectable and honest landlords showed us clean, but rather dismal, dark apartments inside the old buildings. Being in emotional need of naturally lit living spaces myself, I understood Lily and Hudson seeking out those environments to soothe their souls. Lily told me that part of the attraction of even the Vancouver warehouse was its big windows close to the ceiling which sent broad rays of light across its wooden floors.

Finally a landlord we came to know as Lying Marla returned our call. Lily's heart was set on the huge studio Marla was renting out with a wonderful sunny bay window in a building quite near Concordia University. (When I had asked Lily if she wanted to live close enough to walk to classes, she replied jauntily that she wanted to be close enough to walk in heels.) We both imagined how homey Lily could make Lying Marla's studio once some promised renovations were complete. Marla said the last guy didn't want a stove but that she'd, of course, get Lily one. And she vowed the rusted sink would be replaced and the last tenants' garbage would be removed. And — don't worry, she said — the babies in the baby daycare upstairs, who we could hear bawling in French and English, were relocating. This was the first on our maybe list — until the next landlord warned us to beware of Marla's buildings. Lily, in love with the bay windows, argued, "Come on, Mom, that guy just wants to justify charging more money for his boring, quiet building with no loud music allowed." I convinced Lily that before saying yes to Marla, we should hang around her building like vagrants, harassing the current tenants to give us the lowdown. The owner of the baby daycare, who wasn't relocating, and several other drug dealer-looking types were only too anxious to tell us that we should forget any renovations happening or even stoves showing up. Lying Marla never comes through.

The humidity and the frustrating hunt were making Lily and me bicker while I swerved the rental car around Montreal pedestrians who haphazardly wandered into the streets. Lily and I both tried to subdue our exhilaration when we entered another historic building, this one with beautifully tiled, well-lit halls. A pleasant young apartment manager led us to a studio that she cautioned we would find small (bigger would cost considerably more). She neglected to say that it was smaller than most dog houses. I wanted to cry like the babies in the baby daycare imagining where I might be leaving Lily.

That night, Lily had a horrible nightmare and woke me from my restless sleep to say maybe it was all a mistake, that she wasn't ready for university and living in this unfamiliar French city for four years. Stressed and on edge, I called Will in the morning and poured out the details of our wretched apartment hunt, as well as Lily's nightmare-induced apprehension.

At my insistence, the next morning, Lily and I tried a crepe restaurant, whose enticing scent of browning sugar was no indication of the lackluster fare inside. With her uneaten breakfast in a take-out box, Lily and I perched on a bench in a church courtyard so she could check for replies to Craigslist enquiries on her phone. She craned her neck upward, looking toward the blue sky.

"Mom, what if I can't do this? What if the exams are hard?" A long pause. "What if the guys are different? What if they expect more?"

Focus, I told myself. Help her past this. "It might be hard, but you'll study. And, look, you've met lots of guys. Guys are guys.

Only some are dicks. Keep your guard up. Don't take risks. You'll find the nice ones." I realized I needed to be her cheerleader; she had been just a kid during her previous exploits, and probably a lucky one. Maybe by going to classes, getting her own apartment, and living away from us, Lily really was starting over again. Moments later, I shared a text with her from her dad. "Bring her home," he had written. "She has to want to be there." In a typical overarching male way, Will was solving our problems.

"Tell Dad I'm okay," Lily insisted now. "Tell him it was just a middle-of-the-night thing." She handed her take-out box to a street person in the corner of the churchyard. The two of them nodded at each other.

Will responded to my reassuring text, "If Lily is SURE she is going to stay, try upping our targeted budget for monthly rent." The global economic decline had made everyone skittery around money, but Will's advice was what we needed to turn the corner on our dismal hunt. As Lily and I followed Will's business-like, less emotional advice, changing our search perimeters slightly, the situation improved accordingly, until finally we found what could be the answer to our apartment-hunting dreams.

A brilliant Toronto firm had completely overhauled a downtown building and turned it into a student residence type of accommodation, with no connection to the universities. It truly was quite incredible for a private building, containing a welcoming lobby with games and a big screen TV, common study areas with wireless, a commercial size laundry facility, and — incredibly — a soundproof room for student bands to practice in. There were other big perks — details Lily, having lived without even hot water a year ago, didn't yet appreciate, but I was certain would grow on her — like dishwashers and air conditioning in the contemporary, furnished, ceramic-tiled suites. So the drawback? The rooms weren't individual. This firm rents you a share of a four-bedroom apartment. Each bedroom locks, but you get up in the morning to have breakfast with three strangers. These strangers, however, might act very much like you, as the student-aged managers have you fill out a seven-page questionnaire covering details like: your level of cleanliness (obsessive for Lily), how many hours you sleep (not enough) and study (lots, I hoped), what music you like (vastly important to my daughter), what teams you root for, if any (nope), and how often you party or want others to party (most weekends). With this info, they match you to your roommates. The psychology of it fascinates me, but did Lily want to live with three other Lily's? It was a hundred times better than the best we'd seen, but still Lily was nervous about committing. "Please, Mom, I have one last place typed in my phone. Can we just go see it?" Wiping the sweat off the back of my neck, I traipsed down St. Catherine Street behind her.

Once more we were met by a pretty twenty-something manager — this one in a tidy linen suit — hired to show the suites of a four-storey building and, I assumed cynically now, to gain our trust. She told us the building was originally a house built one hundred and twenty years ago. Lily found it charming and properly bohemian. I found it old and smelling like the gas stove leaked. But it wasn't under the freeway and the kitchen wasn't in a closet, and, unlike others we viewed, if any chubby friends came over, they would fit into the bathroom without having to go use the one in the Chinese restaurant next door. Incredibly, it had three rooms — a bedroom, a galley kitchen/living space big enough for half a couch, and a bathroom — and looked out over the busy Boulevard De Maisonneuve. Lily stood behind the manager and gave me a silent thumbs-up. "It's noisy," I said, aware of the sounds of traffic, clipping heels, and a half dozen conversations outside.

"I grew up in the 'burbs, Mom. Now I want to fall asleep to street noises." Miss Lovely Manager promised they would re-enamel the chipped sink and tub, and fix the broken light. She added that the missing carpet in the hallway was being replaced all the way up the two flights of winding stairs (which would prove to be a lie). Being so close to a decision, my breath was jagged again — or maybe I was just about to pass out from the heat in yet another steamy building with one hundred and twenty-year-old insulation. I was leaning toward the contemporary psych experiment — though it had the potential to be the set for a reality TV show. It was modern and well equipped, and I was influenced by the fact that I wouldn't have to imagine Lily alone and lonely. But I did understand her desire for freedom and something that was her own space. I decided I would trust Miss Lovely Manager on the basis that outside, in the four feet of garden between the building's small stoop and the busy boulevard, someone had planted a circle of violet petunias and was caring for them in the oppressive heat. Leaning against the chipped counter, I took many deep breaths and signed the papers. I called Will on my cell to update him as we headed to Rue Crescent and our new favourite Montreal Italian place for lunch, Lily almost skipping ahead of me. As Lily meticulously cut the fat off her prosciutto, I began to explain to her how to properly make my meat sauce.

We found the apartment in August and flew back to Calgary together for Lily to finish her summer serving job at a local pub and for us all to languish in the last dog days of summer. It wasn't just Lily who was leaving though. Cole's summer job was over and he was on his way back to university in Vancouver. Hudson was at home but making rapid plans to vacate the nest as well, though he accompanied us when we took a red-eye flight back to Montreal to set up Lily. After attempting to get back his lost sleep in the rental car in the Ikea parking lot (while I was studying other mother/daughter interactions and Lily was checking out the twenty-nine dollar desks and twelve dollar lamps), he uncomplainingly helped carry the goods up two flights of stairs to her tiny apartment and put the Aspvik and the Leirvik together with only two cold showers to stop his Alberta blood from boiling in the late August heat. Having made the mistake of passing on an Ikea mattress out in the suburbs, we found it impossible to find one in downtown Montreal, and while our search continued, we slept on air mattresses from Canadian Tire. On the third day after we arrived, Will flew in for the

September long weekend, promising to whisk me away from my restless sleep in the stifling apartment to an air-conditioned hotel room. Will and I wanted to kick back and enjoy a tête-à-tête and some joie de vivre over aperitifs on the café patios of Rue Crescent, giving Lily an opportunity to rendezvous on St. Denis with its je ne sais quoi appeal while she had Hudson to watch out for her. But Hudson has never been any better than the rest of us at reining Lily in.

The first serious argument I had with Lily in Montreal happened when I discovered that she hadn't followed Hudson in from a late, late night skateboarding session and was out riding alone at two a.m. while he and I tossed on our air mattresses in the heat. To make matters more alarming, upon her return, she happily told us she'd been talking to some dudes out there and, upon mentioning that she was looking for a cheap bike, they took her to a friend's workplace at a nearby restaurant. Their waiter buddy, they said, put together bikes as a side business. Pressing cold washcloths on my face and neck, it took me more than an hour to stop lecturing my barely adult daughter on her lack of judgment and naivety.

While Will and I sipped our icy drinks during what was supposed to be a pleasant soiree in a Rue Crescent café, he said that he didn't know if he could do it; he wasn't sure he could actually leave Lily in Montreal. "I know she did that stint in Vancouver, but she ended up with Zoë and Cole, thank God. And yeah, sure, she lived without us in Rome at sixteen," he said, his cowboy boot drumming nervously against the patio floor, "but she still had that host family keeping track of her."

"And she travelled Europe last year," I added, with the selfish desire to make him relax enough for me to enjoy watching the stream of tourists, students, and well-dressed locals pass by on the infamous old street.

"Travelling is different," he went on, "and the two of you convinced me, whether it was true or not, that she'd be meeting up with people every step of the way. This time, she's on her own. You know what I mean," he insisted, "it will just be her, living here alone. In Quebec. How did that happen? When Zoë went away to school — one province away, not four — she got a roommate."

We'd been over this all before. Even though we'd had to increase our budget, rent was still cheap in Montreal compared to Vancouver. Still, Cole had also convinced us to let him live on his own when he found a deal of a student apartment in Vancouver. But there was more to Will's how did that happen. With Hudson moving to the coast with his band, Will and I would once more, after twenty-four years of almost always living with children, be on our own. Alone, together, without them.

As we listened to inebriated McGill and Concordia students shouting out to each other, he wondered out loud if Lily was aware of the Mafia presence in Montreal and how to get her to obediently read the cautionary book, Gavin de Becker's The Gift of Fear, the way Zoë had when asked. That comment was the coup de grace to our joie de vivre. We wanted to get back to the sanctuary of our cool hotel room away from the mounting noises of the street.

Lily texted me as we entered the lobby. "Hey Mom, can Hud and I come watch a movie with you guys and check out your mini-bar — lol?" Will was so relieved to have them there with us, especially his eighteen-year-old baby, that he invited them to find a space on our king-size bed and choose the flick. Lily fluffed up the gigantic pillows between us while Hudson kept more of a manly distance, staking out room at the foot of the wide bed. "What say we order a pizza?" Will said, content with his two youngest nearby.

"Daddy, can it be pepperoni? Pepperoni on top of the cheese, please."

Will and Hudson groaned the same father-son sound and insisted she call in the order. I tried not to miss Cole and Zoë just then, to just be happy to have the other two so close.

During those few days together, we toured Old Montreal, weaving around horse-drawn carriage tours and strolled through

Montreal's Little Italy where Lily stocked up on olive oil and bought a leafy basil plant for her windowsill. Lily proclaimed that she loved Montreal. "Word," Hudson said.

"Word," I told them and they grinned at each other, rolling their eyes in unison. Hudson said often during his five-day visit that he should live there. I didn't want to appear too excited, too helicopter-y, but he even said if he went back to school, he would like to go there. Hudson's upcoming adventure was to move from our home in Calgary to Vancouver, where he'd share a house with his band members. He and I were leaning against the rental car while Lily and Will went up to the apartment to take measurements for a piece of wood to add security to the sliding window, when Hudson got the call he'd been waiting for. His crew had found a place. It was far from the action of downtown Vancouver and was going to cost more than they hoped (and likely more than they would discover they could afford), but despite that, he was elated. "That sounds great," I said. "Wow."

Wow, indeed. Screw all that talk of hovering and helicopter-ing and bubble wrap. Our kids were all leaving us. Lily and I saw Hudson and Will off at the airport, and I wobbled over my decision to spend seven more days in Montreal. Of course, there were still tasks I wanted to assist Lily with: setting up an account for her to pay her utility bills, buying some groceries — condiments, vitamins, canned goods, and cleaning supplies — tackling a few simple cooking lessons that I should have covered during the past eighteen years, and arranging for an internet connection, which hadn't got any less complicated or expedient since Zoë started university six years earlier. I know that Lily is a detail person, and she could have managed all that on her own more efficiently than her older siblings. But the real reason for my prolonged stay was that I couldn't bear to leave Lily alone in that small, hot apartment before she had made a few contacts with potential friends. I'd wondered if a week would be long enough for that. Then again, it was only on our second night in Montreal that she had met the bike-building waiter, who appeared to be a nice boy, not a member of the Montreal Soprano family at all. The night before her first day of classes, going against my boring motherly advice to get some sleep, she had me drop her at the apartment of friends of friends of hers from Calgary, who were in Montreal to attend McGill University. She bounced back in at one a.m. to find me reading on her little couch and told me that they were good guys who had given her tight advice about the city, and she was sure to hang out with them again. This ease at meeting people was what I wanted, right?

Universities in the west have distinct campuses, but McGill and Concordia are right in the centre of Montreal. When Lily put on her little black summer dress — a French dress, she decided — and was taken out by her Calgary connections, I left the apartment in search of a breeze and found the streets full of students. Feeling terribly alone in my dotage, I knew I needed to get back home to Calgary.

We had one more sweltering weekend to spend together. It was almost too freaking hot in the apartment to think of using the toaster, let alone conduct cooking lessons over the gas stove, so we sought out air-conditioning once more. Concordia students were everywhere, and the server who brought us our quesadillas in the Mexican restaurant around the corner turned out to be a classmate who invited Lily to go cliff jumping in the Eastern Townships on Sunday. Mon Dieu. I wanted to tag along, not to jump off a cliff, but to sightsee — just the name Eastern Townships sounded like a good time. "I'm on," Lily told the handsome server, with the stipulation that she had to be back for the Italian Club barbecue on Sunday afternoon.

Lily already had photography homework for her black-and-white class and rushed out to shoot a roll of film with a classmate on Saturday. In search of air-conditioning, I took myself to a movie and saw Mamma Mia — alone. Lily checked in with me all weekend, texting me to see what part of St. Catherine Street I might be wandering along. "What's up, Mom? Want to meet at that wrap and café au lait shop on Boulevard De

Maisonneuve when I'm done in the darkroom?" I'd decided that the cooking lessons would be on an as-needed basis from Calgary over the phone or internet.

I knew Lily would have her lonely times. Hudson had told her, in a way that made me feel melancholy, that it was having family around that she would miss — someone coming into your room late at night to find the car keys or waking you up to borrow a CD, and your other sibling's friends hanging out, even if yours have gone home. "You'll even miss Mom bugging you to do things, to clean up your mess, or to bring her car back," he said.

I would be lonely, too, but I probably wouldn't miss their messes or them using my car. There had been more than a few annoying nights during the summer when Hudson and Lily went out to the pub after working late restaurant shifts and came home even later with friends, all of whom were full of midsummer giddiness. As more cars pulled up with stereos blaring, I had worried the racket was going to wake their dad. Thank God, we have extremely tolerant neighbours. On those nights, I thought, fine, I can handle September with all of them away, pissing off roommates rather than their parents.

While Lily slept in her new bed in Montreal (we had finally found the mattress shop), her blond hair spread over her Ikea pillows, I remembered her telling me once, when she was about six, that she wanted to have lots of kids, too, but that she would have them all far apart so that the older ones could look after the babies and she could have her career without them bothering her. I probably reassured her that my babies didn't bother me, even if I acted as if they did sometimes. I certainly would not have been thinking back then of the other disadvantage: if you have them all in a cluster, they might leave you all at once, too.

I'd never been to the movies alone, but it had been a relief that afternoon to sit in the cool theatre and wonder how many of the mothers and daughters we'd seen at Ikea had made it to Mamma Mia to hear Meryl Streep sing ABBA songs and to drool over Pierce Brosnan. Or maybe the daughters, like mine, were making tentative bonds with new acquaintances while their moms were sitting somewhere nearby in the dark listening to Streep's character croon to her twenty-year-old daughter about time slipping through her fingers and all the places she had planned for them to go.

Finally, on Sunday afternoon, the weather broke. The sky turned a steel blue and the rains came. Lily was only a few blocks away at a classmate's apartment using the internet. A stubborn throwback child, Lily still shot film and, in the last six months, she'd resurrected our record album collection from the boxes in the basement. She'd found a cheap record player in a narrow shop selling electronics manufactured before she was born. I imagined that after I left Montreal, her new friends might gather at her place and put one of my old records, which she'd carefully packed amongst her clothes, on her retro turntable and sing along to Fleetwood Mac or Billy Joel while they hung their heads out the window to see who was going by.

Zoë and Cole had good friends in Vancouver now, people who would look out for them and invite them into the story of their lives. I had gotten used to them living away from home, but I couldn't imagine how much I'd miss my youngest two and the commotion they brought to the house.

Occasionally over the past summer months, on mornings after Hudson had partied with friends, he would text me, "Hey, want to buy me breakfast? I don't work till three." How could I refuse? During those breakfasts, he shared more than at other times, letting me in on what his latest plans were. Since high school, Lily would stretch across the back of our living room couch in the afternoon sun, like a sleepy feline, and share what was on her mind. Or we would go out to our favourite coffee/nacho shop. I couldn't solve all of their teenage and young adult angst. Sometimes, it just reminded me of my own. But I had learned to be less afraid of their troubles and just listen, trying not to yap back too much but to guide them with careful assurances that they would find their paths and their passions. Just be careful to leave doors open, I would say. It was all about those open doors.

Preparing to leave Lily in Montreal, I wasn't worried about those sessions of listening and measured advice ending. In some form or another, they would go on. But I already missed hearing her laugh out loud alone in her bedroom and sneaking around naked upstairs because she likes to. I missed her phoning me on my cell with the pretense of spending time together but really wanting to meet up so I would buy her one little thing, which somehow, in her youngest child mind, did show that I loved her. If it were possible, I would have said, "No, Lily, you can't have that thing, but instead I will buy you a thousand pieces of my love." Already I missed the girl she was right then, at that place in time, because I knew she would come home to us and never quite be that Lily again.

Finally, it was the night before I was to leave her in Montreal and return home. Back in Calgary, Hudson was finishing up a small contract to assist with the first stages of the dismantling of our house. Soon he would be packing up, preparing to leave for Vancouver in just a few days. I was folding my clothes to pack in my suitcase. Lily and I had spent the day together shopping for supplies for her photography classes. We found a camera store in Old Montreal that still supported analog cameras and darkroom work. An elderly clerk searched for film, lupes, and static-free cloths for Lily, commenting that he appreciated that her school still time-traveled backward so the students could learn this art.

I had made us a supper of roast chicken, too sticky risotto, and grilled zucchini cakes. I gave her more verbal directions on housekeeping while I packed — I know you won't want to spend much money at the laundry mat, but you have to separate your whites from your darks, or you'll hate your whites. Fruit might seem expensive in the winter but not compared to the price of a fast-food meal, so choose the fruit. I had imagined us finding time for a last stroll down St. Catherine Street, but Lily was reading homework on the history of photography. I could see her nodding to sleep and so suggested she read out loud to me, and together we learned about the camera obscura, the daguerreotype, and Henry

Fox Talbot. She finished up and fell asleep stretched across the bed in her clothes. I tried to concentrate on reading my novel. It was an intriguing one at a suspenseful point, which was good because each time my mind wandered to thoughts of leaving the next day, I felt my chest tighten.

When this stubborn daughter of mine ran off to Vancouver, she was heading for a city both Cole and Zoë lived in. She knew if she needed them, they would have her back. And they did. I held out hope that the Lily with whom I'd wandered the streets of Montreal was a different sort of girl, prepared to begin university and to grow up so far from the rest of us. Thinking of the distance that would stretch between Lily and our family for the better part of four years, I felt the beginning of the type of panic I experience in windowless rooms and tight spaces. I didn't want my mind to go there just yet.

I'd already decided to remind her that her first trip home would come soon and before she knew it, the first term would be over. I thought of all the photos she would take and print between then and now, and of all the images I would create of her in my mind on lonely afternoons, as fall turned to winter. I wanted to put down my book and creep into her bedroom to lie beside her, the way she did with us as a little girl, climbing into our bed night after night. Instead, I hung my head out the window and listened to the students up late, calling out to each other as they passed by, excited by their new independence.

Lily didn't need me there. It was time to go home.

Chapter 17

The House Halfway Up the Hill

Remember that the best relationship is one in which your love for each other exceeds your need for each other.

– the Dalai Lama

Like many empty-nesters, I was hopeful that the complete chaos of taking our family home apart would distract me from its emptiness.

Only two families had ever lived in our house in Calgary and I was a member of both. It was my parents' family home from 1967, the year I began grade three, until Will and I bought it from them in 1990, the year Lily was born. After our kids left, Will and I had weakly considered moving closer to the city centre where his firm's offices are. I had gone as far as to peruse the websites of a couple realtors and look at houses online for a few months, but when it came down to it, I wasn't ready to leave our home, built halfway up the hilly street I'd grown up on, and I knew that the more sentimental of our four kids wouldn't like it either. Lily had confessed that she'd once gotten into an argument with Cole over which of them would buy the house and large shady property from their dad and me when we were, in her words, *too old* and needed to move out.

The renovation got underway while I was in Montreal getting Lily settled. Cole, back to studying film production in Vancouver, was organizing his own apartment, having moved out of Zoë's house. He had borrowed Zoë's boyfriend's truck and did Ikea solo, though we did connect by cell — him in the Richmond, BC, store surrounded by UBC and Simon Fraser University students, and Lily and me among the McGill and Concordia students in the Ikea in Saint-Laurent, Montreal. "Cole, did you see those little stools for plants? If your apartment bathroom is as puny as your sister's, that would make a cheap shelf."

"Yeah, yeah, totally," he said, impatient with the crowds. "I need a shower curtain, but do you have to buy those rings separately? And where do you find the hanging dresser jobs for the closet? It all seems cheap, but it's going to add up at the till, right?" Cole was carefully counting his loonies. He had to be aware of the financial advantage his little sister had by having me right there, as she convinced me that the bamboo plant and decorative mosquito netting would make her hovel *sweet*.

Zoë had been back in her Vancouver home since mid-August, tending to a patch of pumpkins and sunflowers in their small yard and helping her architecture student boyfriend paint the tiny loft he'd ingeniously added to their bedroom. Once again, she had a tutorial assistant position at UBC, instructing students the same age as her siblings in first year art while she completed her Masters. Hudson was adding to his savings by packing (or perhaps a better word is *cramming*) what his siblings had designated as their most precious possessions into storage boxes, labelling them carefully as *Cole's Shit* or *Zoë's Shit*, and smashing down some of the bedroom walls. I did wonder if his contemplative soul would find taking an sledgehammer to the family home difficult, though the experience could be used as material for his rap lyrics, but mostly he was just stoked over his upcoming move with his band to the house they'd found in North Vancouver. It had been difficult to secure. We had figured Hudson and four other twenty-year-olds would have trouble finding a place, unless it was some derelict house in a sketchy neighbourhood. Instead, they ended up in North Van with a big house in an area that Hudson described as *better than yours*.

On my return from Montreal, I had climbed into Will's car at the Calgary airport with the sticky humidity of Montreal far behind me, though still holding onto the image of leaving Lily on the corner of rue Sainte-Catherine and rue Bishop and watching her stride off in the fifth or sixth outfit she'd considered, to her class on the psychology of social deviance. Will turned the car heater on low. As we drove down the Deerfoot, we chatted about the renovation. Will told me they had unearthed *Cowboy and Indian* wallpaper from the sixties in what had been my older brother's bedroom. More recently, that bedroom had been Cole's and decorated with posters of snowboarding and hot girls.

"So, was she okay?" Will had finally asked as we turned off the Deerfoot and onto Southland Drive.

"You mean with me leaving? Of course. We even had a squabble this afternoon in front of a clerk in the bookstore. We were both hungry and cranky."

"But you think she'll be okay?"

I knew that Will and I worried about her being okay in different ways. While he was likely considering her ability to stay safe and take care of her studies, I was worried about her being homesick and lonely for her siblings. "We made up, of course. At lunch. She got silly and told me all the ways she would miss me — like my doing her dishes, telling her not to stay out on a school night, and cooking her eggs while she showered."

Maybe it was the prospect of my leaving and her upcoming freedom, but she had sat back in her chair in the little bistro and almost sang out, "And your painted summer toenails, I'll miss those, and your waking up from the squeaky apartment door opening, I'll definitely miss that, and your opening my neighbour's apartment door by mistake, twice, *that* I will miss." I didn't share that list with Will.

It wasn't until we pulled up in front of our house that I remembered that we'd had the gigantic evergreen felled while I was gone. My mom had planted it when my parents had first bought the house in 1967. "I can't look," I said. "Seriously, I don't think I can bear to look." I was thinking about how Zoë used to climb up through that tree's rough branches until she was higher than the two-storey house. I thought Will was just being kind as he hefted my bags from the trunk and said not to worry, that the view of the house was almost better, but he was being truthful. Now we could see the huge billowy lilacs fronting the house; even the saucer-sized pink and purple hollyhocks were in full splendid view. Could I make an analogy of this? The tree had sheltered the house like I had sheltered my kids. Sheltered? I had tried. But not so much lately, I thought. Not for a while.

Hudson had me take him for breakfast the next morning, and over his *Hungry Guy Special* and my BLT, he told me again how he couldn't wait to get to Vancouver. *His* yard even had an old tennis court in it, he said. (None of them play tennis.) This would be the second time Hudson had taken up residence with a group of his friends in the type of posh neighbourhood that wouldn't normally have young kids renting. In Victoria, he had lived with a mix of students. I remembered the warm fall afternoon when I climbed up onto the roof of his Victoria home where he and his roomies liked to perch, distinguishing themselves from the elderly residents all around them. This time, he would be moving in with his band members (musicians and singers — he was the sole rapper). As he dumped more ketchup on his eggs and told me how big the yard was, I had visions of the Beatles writing and rehearsing on an English country estate. Look out neighbours, I thought.

During the following days, I offered him all the mismatched furniture that was being hauled out of the rooms soon to be renovated and continually waved beer steins, old pots, and more-than-gently used towels and camp chairs at him. Take this. You can have this. How about all these?

"Sure, Mom, I'll see," he'd say. In his final days in Calgary, he had taken to sleeping in before being roused to help demolish a wall or fill in a ditch with newly buried utility lines, and then staying out until the night had been fully squeezed of its entertainment value. Late on a Sunday night, his good friend, and soon-to-be housemate, came over to help fill the rented U-Haul with Hudson's belongings. Without telling us, the two boys had decided to haul the trailer to the outskirts of the city, where his buddy lived with his parents, right then at eleven p.m. rather than during the morning rush hour.

"Give them whatever instructions you have on pulling that thing," I blubbered at Will.

"They're going now?" he said, as unprepared as I was, and started in about turning wide, taking it slow, and other words of advice I don't think he was really concentrating on. We were both hit hard with our new reality. Hudson was going. They'd all left. We were stunned really, hugging this last kid. We held our collective breath while Hudson pulled out around Will's sports car, the overloaded U-Haul bouncing as it left the curb.

Will and I didn't talk much as we got ready for bed, brushing our teeth in a bathroom that would soon be remodeled like so much else in our lives. We got into bed and each took up a book. I noticed that he wasn't turning the pages of his. Me neither. Just then Hudson phoned. He'd forgotten his iPod and was going to take city transit back to get it. He'd sleep at home and join his friend again in the morning. "Go to sleep though, Mom," he said. "We can say goodbye again tomorrow."

Hudson, my most deep-thinking child, was leaving home for what he hoped was the last time. The next morning, I was, of course, happy to drive him to meet his ride out of Calgary, this one horse city of a million plus people. A close friend of his and fellow band member owned the car they would drive through the Rocky Mountains to their newly rented home in North Vancouver. Zoë, a five year resident now of Vancouver, was sure the boys had made a big mistake. "They can't live there, Mom. North Van isn't like moving to Vancouver, like they wanted. The sweet places are all over here near Commercial; that's where they'll want their band to play. And you can't even get back to the north side on public transit at night after the sea ferry stops at ten p.m., which is insane."

I looked at Hudson on the seat beside me, rolling his window down to catch an early morning breeze, so content even in his sleep-deprived state. Cole had managed to find his Vancouver apartment only because of a connection with a good friend of ours and reported back that the rental market was sewn up tight. He had worn his waiter clothes from his summer job — black pants and a white dress shirt — to meet landlords. When Hudson was looking for a place, Cole told me, "No one is going to rent to five twenty-year-olds. If they're lucky, Hudson and his peeps might find a dive, something sketchy, an old grow-op or whatever." Cole was right. Hudson's crew had been shunned again and again until they stopped looking within Vancouver proper. Now they were bursting with pleasure at their score: a *dope* five-bedroom house on the mountain in North Vancouver with a tennis court in back.

"Leave him alone," I had told both Zoë and Cole. "They'll figure it all out." But would I be able to take my own advice that last morning and let him enjoy the beginning of his great adventure? Rush hour traffic was lining up at the major intersections. We sat at a red light, cars humming beside us and the guy on Hudson's CD singing about dreamers within dreams. I took a deep breath and said, "I've told you not to wash your underwear with your dishtowels, right?"

"A dozen times," he replied.

"And to change the bathroom hand towel after you have a bunch of people over?"

"Yeah, yeah. Okay."

"I didn't pay attention to either of those tips until I was twice your age. I just didn't want to pay for more than one load of clothes at the laundry mat. Still, it makes sense to separate it."

Oh my God, where was my brain? What could I tell him that was important and profound, that he might repeat one day to his children? *To thine own self be true? Do unto others as you'd have them do unto you?* The clock was ticking. I only had a few more miles to give Hudson, the master of philosophy, the reader of Gandhi, Siddhartha, and the Dalai Lama, a new way of looking at his state of being. My mind was blank.

"Mom, you need to change lanes, and you're driving ten kilometers under the speed limit."

He was going to end our crucial time together by criticizing my driving (again). I'd show him. "Did I ever tell you," I said, my mind still a vacuum, "not to put grease down the drain? It can really mess up the plumbing." He nodded his head, slowly, as if he was possibly considering the profoundness of my words. Maybe he thought it was an analogy for something more weighty and significant.

I could do better. "Hudson, I read this somewhere — and Zoë says it's helped her — when you are feeling down, try to act the way you want to feel." Hudson looked at me and nodded, a grin on his face. He didn't have to act just then.

We arrived at his friend's home. His teenage sister was saying, in a teary voice that neither boy seemed to notice, "I'm glad Mom had to leave for work and isn't going to see you pull away." Hudson's friend was packing a tall piece of bamboo in a bronze gift bag into his twenty-year-old car. "My mom and dad gave me this plant last night. It brings good luck."

"Sweet," Hudson said.

"*Dope,*" said the teary sister.

Damn, I thought, why hadn't I skipped the advice and just bought bamboo?

Okay, okay, I have to confess, this is not entirely what happened. I left out a part. After I imparted the domestic advice, our conversation went off the rails in a manner I'd promised myself I would prevent.

I had asked Hudson the night before to wake me half an hour before he wanted to leave and I would drive him to his friend's, but exhausted from the headiness of packing up his life, he had slept in. He woke me late for the offered ride, then was impatient while I showered in a daze and got dressed. We'd only gone a few blocks before he put on a CD and started grinning to himself, so happy to be setting off on this venture. *Don't*, I told myself, *do not* ruin this. Resist telling him one more time that he still needs to find a way to make a living above the minimum wage.

We were doing okay. I shared my laundry and mood-lifting advice, and then, registering his exuberant frame of mind, thought I could risk asking him to contact me for *my* sake. I knew I needed to change lanes, but I was too focused on saying that a phone call or even just a short text message would mean *not that he was a child* but that he was *adult* enough to recognize how important that would be to me.

Because of his blissful state, he reacted playfully by using what he thought was a similar tone to mine. "Look, Mom, just because you are a *mom*, you can still listen to me when I tell you to drive properly. It doesn't mean you're less of a mom, just less of a driver, if you fail to signal before you turn into the lane you should have already been in."

Okay, no more advice, I decided. We would have been fine, but just as we were taking the Sarcee overpass, he opted to tell me that the one girl who would be living with them — his friend's girlfriend — was being supported by her parents who were paying her first few months' rent. Hudson had no such expectations of us. He'd been saving up over the summer at home. So why did I have to point out that this girl's situation was different than his? She had never moved out before and her parents, who I'd spoken to at their last band gig, believed that this move represented a gap in her education, not a replacement for it. And that was how we arrived back at that nasty word — *education*. "Don't even talk to me about university," he said.

"I said *education*, not university, just training for something other than working in a coffee shop for ten dollars an hour." I'd said it all enough times to recognize my pattern and to know that the ten dollars an hour comment was something he never wanted to hear again.

"Mom, more than half of the freaking world lives on way less than ten dollars an hour."

"Yeah, well, you might have to move to that part of the world then."

"You know what? I might do that."

"Look, all I'm saying…" I think it was then that he turned the volume up on the song that was playing so neither of us could hear each other. I turned it down. "Hudson, I just don't want you to be underemployed."

"I'm not as materialistic as you," he said and turned the volume up again.

I'd give him that — money didn't burn a hole in the pocket of his Levis. He was quite frugal and wasn't much of a consumer beyond a good iPod and a supply of reading material. Well, I suppose he liked his computer, guitar, and electric keyboard, and didn't mind purchasing a new hoodie and running shoes every so often. It made me think of Steve Martin's character, Navin, in the movie *The Jerk*, who claims to not need anything but then starts in on an ever-expanding list of things he needs. Now I was the one grinning, but I didn't dare share my private association of Hudson with Navin R. Johnson. Twenty-year-old Hudson was thrilled to be trading all the amenities of our home, including groceries and a car to use, for a house in North Vancouver with four friends, no car, and a fridge they'd have to fill themselves, not to mention household bills to pay.

I didn't want him to think I was against the band. I wasn't. Hudson looked away from me, staring out the side window. The sun was shining. It was still the soft autumn morning during which I'd promised myself not to argue his immediate life choices. His dad and I couldn't always make out the words while Hudson rapped, but when we read them on paper, we saw they were literary and, not surprisingly, profound. Would rap ever pay Hudson's bills or buy his groceries? *Did it matter that morning?*

Hudson and I both stopped our nonsense when we turned the corner into his friend's neighbourhood. We stood beside his buddy and his buddy's sad sister, and I hugged Hudson and he hugged me back long and solid. I knew he put a lot into that hug. I knew also that I wouldn't hear from him much once he headed down the highway and took up residence a mountain range away from us.

It was different with each of them. Guarded over the possibility of Lily's first university experience going sour, I was in touch with her almost every day, if not a quick call, then a text or two, as she figured out her classes and made new friends. Even Cole, living alone for the first time and reportedly liking it, wasn't beyond a text to Will or me, shedding light on the meaning of his latest self-directed film for class and telling us how we could view it online. Like Hudson, Zoë could be harder to reach, but she'd befriended me on Facebook and we were sending private messages back and forth with an easy rhythm.

With three kids on the coast and the house in tatters, we planned to fly Lily to Vancouver and all meet up at Zoë's for Thanksgiving. So while I felt Hudson letting go of our tense conversation with his hug, I was glad we would see each other in a few weeks over turkey and pumpkin pie. The hug had helped, but even so, getting through the rest of the day was going to be difficult for me.

I couldn't go home to our house stricken with pre-renovation ugliness. I couldn't face the Bobcat tearing up the lawn and flower beds, and making the neighbours gawk. I suddenly really did have an empty nest. We would also soon have four renovated bedrooms, a family-sized third bathroom, a back entrance big enough for four *kids'* backpacks as well as their skateboards, runners, flip flops, and high heels, and a new window seat that would be just the spot for writing that last minute essay or curling up to text a few friends. Clearly, renovation planning had started in my denial stage. I had insisted that we still needed a house that would accommodate four kids, or at least three (Zoë had lived away for five years already). After all, at that point, two of them were away at universities — it didn't count as moving out if we still assisted with their rent, right?

Now we were partway through September and no one was begging for a last minute ride to school. I had always said I didn't want to *taxi* them, but despite a lack of conversation during the morning car ride, I liked that time, forced to decipher the lyrics of their hip hop CDs while they ate cereal or toast with jam (the girls) or drank protein powder and milk (the boys). I'd drive them and then I'd go for a workout at the gym.

This autumn would be different. No one hanging out on the front lawn after classes. Nobody raiding the fridge, playing pool in our basement, or annoying our neighbours with their rap tunes. Five o'clock to seven o'clock in the evening would be the hardest time to adapt to. It would be so quiet while I made my usual last minute menu decisions and efforts to put dinner on the table for Will and me.

We are a family of six. When the kids were young, Will was rarely home in time to join us for early dinners to accommodate piano lessons, baseball practices, football games, or math tutoring. No problem. I cooked for six anyway. On cold nights, I'd do a roast and vegetables or, in the afternoon, I'd put on a stew. When I was less inspired, I went with spaghetti or butter chicken — cheating with a little package to get it going. In a rush, there were always wraps or a saucy stir fry. (Note to Hudson, my fact checker: I *did* cook nice meals sometimes. I'm certain of it.)

When Zoë moved away for university, there were still five of us. So I cooked for five. The winter Cole took off for Whistler, there were four of us left, the size of an average family. I still had to cook. The September that Hudson started university in Victoria, it was just Will, Lily, and me, and I realized my *cooking threshold*. Three people were — well, sort of like a holiday in my mind. "Hey, there are just the three of us," I'd say. "Let's order a pizza or hunker down in front of the TV with sushi from that place we like."

Now that we were down to two, I wondered how often Will and I would eat grilled cheese sandwiches for dinner. Sure, we'd require sustenance from time to time, but who cooks for two people? I mean, what's the point in that? Clearly, I would have to look at this empty nest "ordeal" more closely. Having had our four kids early, we were the first of our friends to navigate this latest iteration of parenting. I was in transition, but obviously I had some figuring out to do if I was going to lead the way.

I drove to a bathroom fixture store and absently looked at the shiny and new sinks, trying to imagine the pretty glass ones with toothpaste spit or Hudson's brown and Cole's strawberry blonde whiskers in them. I left the bath shop wondering how often their whiskers *would* be in them and, instead of getting into the car, thought about sitting on the curb and crying. There was a homeless guy and his shopping cart spilling over with bottles on the other side of the street. The guy waved at me and smiled, and I waved back and drove away. A few blocks later, I got out of the car to wander into one of my favourite bakeries. Peering into the glass cases of cakes, squares, and cookies, I thought about Hudson's weakness for chocolate chip peanut butter cookies. I bought half a dozen of them to share with my brother, our contractor. Finally, I called my closest friend, a mom with younger kids, and asked if I could come sit on her deck for a while. I brought lattes, and she fed me muffins and listened to my confession of arguing with Hudson against all my best intentions.

I surprised myself by admitting how nervous I was of this stage of our home renovation, taking apart rooms that had worked alright for us for years. I was ignoring the truth. It might have seemed like the excitement of tearing the house up and restructuring it to suit the changes in our lives would keep me going, but I wanted it all back, my kids and my house, and everything I loved about raising a big noisy family in a less-than-perfect space.

Avoiding the first dinner at the kitchen table with just the two of us, Will and I went out for ginger beef and salt-and-pepper seafood, and then a movie, the underwhelming *Get Smart*. Afterward, while he got ready for bed, I sat on the stairs that descended from Lily's and our bedrooms. Yeah, the house would get a bit bigger with the renovation, but we'd end up with one less bedroom. When they all came back home — Christmases, I guessed — we'd utilize a pull-out in the family room until someone's significant other or spouse dictated they needed to visit someone else's parents' family home. The renovated space would suit us all better; we'd replace all the single beds with queens to accommodate those future partners. They'd all be enthusiastic about the family room we had planned for the extra space, and everyone would be happy to wash up in a bathroom that hadn't been converted by Lily into a darkroom. The boys' small bedrooms had a sizable opening in the wall for the one shared window, and on her last visit home, Zoë had complained about the lumpy mattress in her old built-in little girl's bed.

I felt like curling up right then and there *in* Zoë's bed, the way I used to when she first went off to Emily Carr. I thought of Zoë in that room, bent over creating a work of art, her nose almost touching the paper, and the boys when they were small enough to crawl through that space between the windows and then launch themselves onto the bed below, and Lily playing Elvis records in her room only a few weeks ago.

"You forgot to close the bedroom door," Will said, dozing off. He liked it closed. I liked it open. I pictured Lily in Montreal, it would be three a.m. there. Even with the late hours she keeps, I imagined her asleep under her lacy mosquito netting. At midnight in Vancouver, Cole might be up, editing on his computer screen, creating a masterpiece. Zoë keeps late hours, too. Perhaps she'd be watching a movie on TV with her roommates as she marked student gallery reviews. Hudson would still be bouncing his belongings across BC.

"Do you mind if we keep the door open?" I said, climbing in beside Will. It seemed less lonely with it open.

Staring out the window over Will's head at a narrow moon, I wanted to be comforted about the future. I pictured a day when Zoë would be painting a canvas in her studio at UBC, and Cole would be leading a crew of students filming a scene on the rainy streets of East Van. I pictured Hudson alone with his notebook, jumping from rock to rock along Vancouver's North Shore, scribbling words of prose in the lapses of motion... and miles and miles away, Lily starting to feel the eastern cold, stamping her feet to warm them as she lifted an image from a negative bath. Here in Calgary, Will would reach for his Blackberry to text me so I could remind him what evening we'd chosen for *date night*.

Is it possible that the six of us might pause together in our busy lives and cosmically connect, that I'd be working on another draft, gazing out the window at the windy backyard, and suddenly feel them close? I believed it could happen, that there would be days when we all turned inward at the same time and thought of each other and the noise we made together at our house, halfway up the hill, and we would grab our phones and reach out to each other.

"I can do this," I told myself, remembering Lily swinging open the door of the university on St. Catherine Street, her thin figure standing tall as she stepped inside.

Epilogue

Two Years Slip By

Why, sometimes I've believed as many as six impossible things before breakfast.

– *The Queen in* Through the Looking Glass

I'm alone again in the house.

For part of a bright but snowy December and into early January, our home was crowded with our kids and their friends. The detritus of their visit fills the house still — snowboards and old skates in the porch, left-behind scarves draped over chair backs, and take-out Chinese containers leaning against eggnog cartons in the fridge. Once the guys had added their last-minute presents to the mix, the gifts had spilled out under the fresh scotch pine Christmas tree. The deluge of snow lent the holiday an otherworldly atmosphere. Every outing required boots, or at least high tops, to be unearthed from the heap that had collected on the brand new slate tiles at the door. I had learned to keep my favourite gloves hidden from indiscriminate hands. Those who volunteered to shovel the walk risked friendly fire in the form of snowballs tossed at them from the front deck. It had seemed like there was always a friend on the couch or someone trying to find a sibling or the truck keys. The noise had returned with one kid trying to locate the contact lens solution while another called out to see if there was milk in the downstairs fridge.

Now twenty- to twenty-seven-years-old (Zoë's guy), they had generally stayed out late catching up with their Calgary peeps and taken advantage of the break from classes to sleep in like teenagers again, until eleven or noon. All except Cole, who had consistently been the first up and out of the house, filming a crew of snowboarders landing tricks at secret locations on city property. He had anxiously enthused about a new young woman he'd been seeing in Vancouver and shared our family events with her via a stream of texts. With everyone home, plugged-in cellphones had littered our two kitchen counters, and someone had always been looking for a charger. Beeps, tweets, and pings echoed through the house. "Remember what it was like at Inkaneep Resort?" Zoë had said during a noisy dinner when she was chided for misplacing her vibrating phone again. "No phones, no internet, no TV even." When the kids were still in grade school, before my brother built our cottage in the Shuswaps, we'd discovered an idyllic resort — a row of small cabins built in the fifties, along the tree-lined shores of Osoyoos Lake, in southern BC.

"Yeah, but we had the lake," Cole said. "And we weren't afraid to talk ourselves onto other people's boats."

"At night, the adults would build a campfire," Lily explained to Zoë's guy, "but the kids would all go have these epic games of hide-and-seek tag, where the last kid was pursued by the pack into cool places, like under the pier." For a moment, there had been silence. Then a phone had chirped at us from the counter.

"None of you even owned a cellphone then," I'd said. But no one had answered; they had already moved on to discussing a text Hudson had received from a cousin of theirs inviting them to a party. Do Lily, Hudson, Cole, and Zoë reminisce much about that time before cellphones, before texting? I think they can hardly recall it. This is the world they know.

For most of the holiday, we had skipped family breakfast; pre-Christmas, I was finishing gift shopping, and post-Christmas, I was out early to stock the house with provisions. I'd almost forgotten how much the last two decades of my life had revolved around trips to the grocery store. Hudson's sunny new girlfriend, the third of eight kids, provided some perspective; her tales of family meal times made our borderline chaos seem sane.

Most days, Zoë's boyfriend had gotten up and fixed himself and Zoë each a bowl of cold cereal and milk. Hudson liked to make himself a smoothie with fruit and yogurt, while Cole had turned his dad onto tall protein powder shakes to start their days. Only Lily had been consistently thrilled by being asked to wait for me to return, and we'd whip ourselves up hot breakfasts — sausages and scrambled eggs, blueberry pancakes, or a big fat BLT. A few days before the kids were set to leave, I had tracked them down in the evening, in person or by text, and said, "Breakfast together tomorrow at 10:30, okay?"

My scheduling worked: they all humored me and, for the last few mornings, we had sat down for breakfast together. Zoë was more interested in the stacks of pancakes than usual. It had been a marvelous new holiday season for our family — because it was growing again. A few months ago, just before receiving her Masters degree, twenty-five-year-old Zoë and her boyfriend of the last five years had learned that the IUD Zoë used for birth control had failed them. "Got one past the goalie," they were able to jest once we had all passed the initial stress and concern of the IUD being surgically removed without interfering with the tiny new being. Zoë's guy would touch her rounding belly, and we would all grin like Cheshire cats. He was finishing a degree in architecture and was madly planning a renovation of their Vancouver home to accommodate the new baby. It was the twenty-first century — we were all okay with them transitioning to being parents before we helped plan the fun and romantic ocean-side wedding of Zoë's dreams.

For the few weeks that the house had been full, I'd set aside the novel I was working on and the research I'd been doing into superstitions for it. I had told my kids that the challenge was to not incorporate every new superstition I read about into my personal repertoire. "Mom, it must be hard for you to keep that collection of superstitions in your head a closed club," Zoë had teased me. "Are you really impervious to others sneaking in to join the cache already in your brain?"

Brushing the snow off the car before driving Cole to the airport, a blur of white had skidded along the hedge and through the yard. It was a big snowy rabbit, and it tucked itself up against the lilac bush and looked out at me. I'd recently read that a white rabbit in your yard meant either it was a good year to have a child or your garden would be especially fertile that year. Our neighborhood is overrun with rabbits — it would always be a good year to have a child. Okay, Zoë, I had decided, I'll take on this superstition, too.

Cole had been the first to head back, eager to spend New Year's with his new girlfriend. Lily had flown back to Montreal for the start of classes a few days later. She had called me her second day home. "It's so cold, Mom. I can't even hang onto my phone — it's so cold." She had been rushing to a grocery store to buy ingredients for my meat sauce. She called again from the vegetable aisle. "Tell me exactly what you put in yours. I want mine to taste like yours. I just have to have good food here to get through this week. Who's still there? Did Hudson go back?" Hudson and Zoë's guy had become good friends and had loaded up their snowboards and suitcases to head to the airport together the day before. Hudson had decided to try another term of university, in Vancouver this time, where he'd been living in a house not too far from Zoë's.

"Hudson left yesterday. I always use red onions and fresh garlic."

"Do you think Hudson will like school this time?"

"It's so hard to say, Lily."

"What are you and Zoë doing? I wish I was still there hanging out."

Zoë had been commissioned to paint a mural for an Olympic art show but was free to hang back in Calgary for another day and return when the price of flights wasn't as inflated, promising me some mom and daughter time. We had planned to return a maternity shirt that didn't fit her, go out for a peaceful lunch, and, because Calgary was being treated to balmy chinook weather, take a walk along the reservoir. After all the lovely chaos of Christmas, a day of activities devoted to Zoë and me seemed like bliss, but I was aware of the hush Lily had returned to in her small Montreal studio.

"We're not doing much, Lily. It's quiet here. Make your sauce, and call if you need help."

But Lily hadn't been ready to disconnect. "Hey, Mom. How will we work it when Zoë has the baby in June? We'll be there, right? How will we make sure that we're in Vancouver?"

Funny, Cole had asked me something similar. He had no interest in being around the delivery room, but he wanted to be close by "to film the kid as soon as it arrives."

"We'll work it out," I told Zoë's little sister. "It will be summertime. That'll make it easier."

The following day, I took my eldest daughter to the airport, gave her blossoming body a firm hug, and handed her over to security before driving back to this too-quiet, too-calm house. But imagining our first little grandchild, I felt less lonely. The baby's other grandparents live in Calgary as well — and the bright bedroom that was Zoë's pre-renovation now has enough space for a queen bed and a tiny crib when they visit. Suddenly, the renovated house was beginning to make sense again... Despite the miles that separate us, our family was growing and this house, halfway up the hill, is still home.

Word, my kids would say. And so I'll type a message to them all in their faraway places: "Text me. Love, Mom."

Acknowledgements

I truly thank my devoted family and friends who've patiently read my words and edited and critiqued so willingly. My gratitude to the dedicated team at Iguana Books and especially my editor, Kathryn Willms, for her expertise and fine tuning. And thank you to my daughters: Shea, for the beautiful cover, and Rose, for her lovely photo.